Last War of the World-Island

ALEXANDER DUGIN

Last War of the World-Island

The Geopolitics of Contemporary Russia

LONDON
ARKTOS
2015

ΛRKTOS

Arktos.com fb.com/Arktos arktosmedia arktosjournal

© 2015 Arktos Media Ltd.

First English edition published in 2015 by Arktos Media Ltd., originally published as *Geopolitika Rossii* (Moscow: Gaudeamus, 2012).

ISBN
978-1-917646-22-2 (Softcover)

Translation
John Bryant

Editing
John B. Morgan

Layout
Tor Westman

Cover Design
Andreas Nilsson

CONTENTS

Editor's Note

This book was originally published in Russian in 2012. Although the geo-political situation of Russia has changed considerably since then, especially as regards the Ukrainian crisis and the subsequent outbreak of war in east-ern Ukraine, Alexander Dugin has made it clear that he stands by his origi-nal assessment and criticism of Putin's approach, and that only by Russia's assertion of itself as a land-based regional power in opposition to the sea-based Atlanticism of the United States and NATO can Russia survive in any genuine sense.

Footnotes that were added by me are denoted with an "Ed." follow-ing them, and those that were added by the translator are denoted with "Tr." Those which were part of the original Russian text have no notation. Where sources in other languages have been cited, I have attempted to re-place them with existing English-language editions. Citations to works for which I could locate no translation are retained in their original language. Website addresses for on-line sources were verified as accurate and available during the period of April and May 2015.

JOHN B. MORGAN IV
Budapest, Hungary, May 2015

CHAPTER I

Toward a Geopolitics of Russia's Future

Theoretical Problems of the Creation of a Fully-Fledged Russian Geopolitics

The geopolitics of Russia is not the mere application of a geopolitical arsenal to the Russian government. In other words, Russian geopolitics cannot be created from without, as the simple, mechanical application of "universal" laws to a concrete and well-defined object. The problem is that a Russian geopolitics is possible only on the basis of a deep study of Russian society, both its present and its past. Before drawing conclusions about how the Russian government is correlated with territory,[1] we should study Russian society scrupulously and thoroughly in its structural constants and especially trace the formation and evolution of Russians' views about the surrounding world; that is, we should study how Russians understand and interpret the surrounding world and its environment. The problem is not only to learn about the geographical structure of the Russian territories (contemporary or historical); that is important, but insufficient. We must clarify how Russian society understood and interpreted the structure of these ter-

---

[1]   "Territory," "space," or "territorial space" is how the Russian word *prostrantsvo*, equivalent to the German *Raum*, is translated throughout.—Tr.

I

ritories at different times; what it considered "its own," what as "alien," and how the awareness of borders, cultural, and civilizational identity, and the relationship to those ethnoses and *narodi*[2] living in neighboring territories changed. The views of Russian society (on the basis of which the Soviet society and in our time that of the Russian Federation were formed)[3] about territorial space have been insufficiently studied, and as a result this most important factor in the creation of a full-fledged Russian geopolitics is for the moment only available to us fragmentally and episodically.

Further, the question of the attitude of Russian society toward political forms and types of government remains open. If in the Marxist period we were guided by the theory of progress and the shifts of political-economic blocs, and considered the experience of the Western European countries as "universal," then today this reductionist schema is no longer suitable. We must build a new model of Russian sociopolitical history, study the logic of that history, and propose structural generalities that reflect the peculiarities characteristic of our society's relations, at different historical stages, to other governmental and political systems. And in this case, alas, we have but a few relevant works, since Marxist theories yield notorious caricatures, based on exaggerations and violence against the historical facts and especially against their significance. The same is true of the application of liberal Western methods to Russian history and to Russian society.

These difficulties must not dishearten us. The intuitively obvious moments of Russian social history, observations about the peculiarities of Russian culture, and the very structure of the geopolitical discipline can be reference points for the movement toward the creation of a full-fledged

---

2   Dugin uses the term *narodnik* as synonymous with the German term *Volk*, or peoples.—Ed.

3   The author distinguishes between *Russkii* and *Rossiiskii*, which are both used throughout the text. The latter, unlike the former, usually refers to the notion of belonging to a nation-state, the Russian Federation. The former, on the other hand, refers to the broader notion of an ethno-social identity. Although there is no effective way to convey this in English, where possible, I translate the latter with "of the Russian Federation," and otherwise use the term "Russian."—Tr.

Russian geopolitics. Such an approximate representation of Russian society will be enough to begin with.

Geopolitical Apperception

Classical geopolitics (both Anglo-Saxon and European) gives us some fundamental prompts for the construction of a Russian geopolitics. We can accept them unreservedly. However, in this case an important factor interferes, whose significance is great in non-classical physics (both for Einstein and for Bohr), but even more appreciable in geopolitics: the geopolitical system *depends on the position of the observer and interpreter.*[4] It is not enough to agree with the geopolitical features that classical geopolitics attributes to Russia; we should accept those features and view our history and our culture as their confirmation. That is, we should grasp ourselves as products of that geopolitical system. In a word, we should understand ourselves not as a neutral observer, but as an observer embedded in a historical and spatial context. This procedure is usually called "geopolitical apperception."

Geopolitical apperception is the ability to perceive the totality of geopolitical factors consciously, with an explicit understanding of both our subjective position and the regularities of the structure of what we perceive.

The notion of a "Russian geopolitician" does not signify only citizenship and a particular sphere of professional knowledge. It is something much deeper: a Russian geopolitician is an exponent of geopolitical views and the carrier of historical-social and strategic constants that are historically characteristic of Russian society (today, that of the Russian Federation). Geopolitics permits two global positions (Mackinder[5] calls them "the seaman's point of view" and "the landsman's point of view"). One cannot en-

---

4   Alexander Dugin, *Geopolitics* (Moscow: Academic Project, 2011).

5   Halford Mackinder (1861–1947) was an English geographer, and also Director of the London School of Economics. A pioneer who established geography as an academic discipline, he is also regarded as the father of geopolitics.—Ed.

gage with geopolitics if one does not acknowledge these positions. He who occupies himself with it first clarifies his own position and its relation to the geopolitical map of the world. This position is neither geographical nor political (having to do with one's citizenship), but *sociocultural,* civilizational, and axiological. It touches the geopolitician's own *identity.* In certain cases, it can be changed, but this change is as serious as a change of one's religious confession or a radical modification of one's political opinions.

Heartland

Classical geopolitics proceeds from the fact that *the territory of contemporary Russia, earlier the Soviet Union (USSR), and still earlier the Russian Empire, is the Heartland; it is the land-based (telluric) core of the entire Eurasian continent.* Mackinder calls this zone "the geographical pivot of history," from which the majority of telluric impulses historically issue (from the ancient steppe nomads like the Scythians and Sarmatians to the imperial center of Russian colonization in the sixteenth through the nineteenth centuries, or the Communist expansion during the Soviet period). "Heartland"[6] is a typical *geopolitical concept.* It does not signify belonging to Russia as to its government and does not have an exclusively geographical meaning. In it we are dealing with a "spatial meaning" (*Raumsinn,* according to F. Ratzel),[7] which can become the heritage of the society placed on this territory. In this case it will be perceived and included in the social system and will ultimately express itself in political history. Historically, Russians did not immediately realize the significance of their location and only accepted the baton of tellurocracy *after the Mongolian conquests of Ghengis Khan,* whose empire was a model of tellurocracy.

---

6   Halford Mackinder, *Democratic Ideals and Reality* (Washington: National Defence University Press, 1996).

7   Friedrich Ratzel, *Die Erde und das Leben* (Leipzig: Bibliographisches Institut, 1902). Ratzel (1844–1904) was a German geographer and ethnologist who attempted to merge the two disciplines, and is regarded as the first German geopolitical thinker.—Ed.

But, beginning from the fifteenth century, Russia steadily and sequentially moved toward taking on the characteristics of the Heartland, which gradually led to the *identification of Russian society with the civilization of Land, or tellurocracy.* The Heartland is not characteristic of the culture of Eastern Slavs, but during their historical process, Russians found themselves in this position and adopted a land-based, continental civilizational mark.

For that reason, Russian geopolitics is by definition the geopolitics of the Heartland; land-based geopolitics, the geopolitics of Land.[8] Because of this, we know from the start that Russian society belongs to the land-based type. But how Russia became land-based, what stages we traversed along this path, how this was shown in our understanding of territorial space and the evolution of our spatial representations, and, on the other hand, how it has been reflected in political forms and political ideologies, remains to be thoroughly clarified. This puts an *a priori* obligation on Russian geopolitics: it *must* see the world from the position of the civilization of Land.

Russia as a "Civilization of Land"

Here it makes sense to correlate that which falls under "Heartland" and is the core of "the civilization of Land" with the political reality of the contemporary Russian Federation in its existing borders.

This correlation itself is exceedingly important: in making it, we correlate Russia in its actual condition with its unchanging geopolitical *spatial sense* (*Raumsinn*). This juxtaposition gives us a few important guidelines for the construction of a full-fledged and sound Russian geopolitics for the future.

First, we must think of the contemporary Russian Federation in its current borders as *one of the moments* of a more extensive historical cycle, during which Eastern-Slavic statehood self-identified as "the civilization of Land" and became more and more closely identified with the Heartland.

---

8   Alexander Dugin, *Foundations of Geopolitics* (Moscow: Arctogaia, 2000).

This means that contemporary Russia, considered geopolitically, is not something new; it is not just a government that appeared twenty-something years ago. It is merely an episode of a long historical process lasting centuries, at each stage bringing Russia closer and closer to becoming an expression of "the civilization of Land" on a planetary scale. Formerly, the Eastern-Slavic ethnoses and Kievan Rus[9] were only the periphery of the Orthodox, Eastern Christian civilization and were in the sphere of influence of the Byzantine Empire. This alone already put Russians into the Eastern pole of Europe.

After the invasion of the Mongolian Horde, Rus was included in the Eurasian geopolitical construct of the land-based, nomadic empire of Ghengis Khan (later a piece in the West broke off, as the Golden Horde).[10]

The fall of Constantinople and the weakening of the Golden Horde made the great Muscovite Czardom an heir to *two* traditions: the political and religious byzantine one and the traditional Eurasianist one, which passed to the great Russian princes (and later to the Czars) from the Mongols. From this moment, the Russians begin to think of themselves as "the Third Rome," as the carriers of a special type of civilization, sharply contrasting in all its basic parameters with the Western European, Catholic civilization of the West. Starting from the fifteenth century, Russians emerged onto the scene of world history as "a civilization of Land," and all the fundamental geopolitical force-lines of its foreign policy from then on had only one goal: the integration of the Heartland, the strengthening of its influence in the zone of Northeast Eurasia, and the assertion of its identity in the face of a much more aggressive adversary, Western Europe (from

---

9   The Kievan Rus was a Slavic kingdom that emerged in the ninth century, which was comprised of parts of modern-day Russia, Ukraine, and Belarus. It was the first form of government to appear on the territory of Russia. It was conquered by the Mongols in the thirteenth century.—Ed.

10 The Golden Horde was the name given to the empire that arose in the Slavic regions that were conquered by the Mongolians in the thirteenth century (after the color of the Mongolians' tents). This kept the area that later became Russia isolated from developments in Europe.—Ed.

the eighteenth century, Great Britain and, more broadly, the Anglo-Saxon world), which was in the process of realizing its role as "the civilization of the Sea," or thalassocracy. In this duel between Russia and England (and later the United States) there unfolds from then on, from the eighteenth century and until today, the geopolitical logic of world history, "the great war of continents."[11]

This geopolitical meaning remains, on the whole, unchanging in all later stages of Russian history: from the Muscovite Czardom through the Romanov Russia of Saint Petersburg and the Soviet Union to the current Russian Federation. From the fifteenth to the twenty-first century, Russia is a planetary pole of the "civilization of Land," a *continental* Rome.

The Geopolitical Continuity of the Russian Federation

In all the principal parameters, the Russian Federation is the geopolitical heir to the preceding historical, political, and social forms that took shape around the territory of the Russian plain: Kievan Rus, the Golden Horde, the Muscovite Czardom, the Russian Empire, and the Soviet Union. This continuity is not only territorial, but also historical, social, spiritual, political, and ethnic. From ancient times, the Russian government began to form in the Heartland, gradually expanding, until it occupied the entire Heartland and the zones adjoining it.[12] The spatial expansion of Russian control over Eurasian territories was accompanied by a parallel sociological process: the strengthening in Russian society of "land-based" social arrangements, characteristic of *a civilization of the continental type.* The fundamental features of this civilization are:

- conservatism;
- holism;

---

11 Mikhail Leontyev, *The Great Game* (Saint Petersburg: Astrel', 2008).

12 George Vernadsky *A History of Russia* (New Haven: Yale University Press, 1969).

- collective anthropology (the *narod* is more important than the individual);
- sacrifice;
- an idealistic orientation;
- the values of faithfulness, asceticism, honor, and loyalty.

Sociology, following Sombart,[13] calls this a "heroic civilization." According to the sociologist Pitirim Sorokin,[14] it is the ideal sociocultural system.[15] This sociological trait was expressed in various political forms, which had a *common denominator*: the constant reproduction of civilizational constants and basic values, historically expressed in different ways. The political system of Kievan Rus differs qualitatively from the politics of the Horde, and that, in turn, from the Muscovite Czardom. After Peter I,[16] the political system sharply changed again, and the October Revolution of 1917 also led to the emergence of a radically new type of statehood. After the collapse of the USSR there arose on the territory of the Heartland another government, again differing from the previous ones: today's Russian Federation.

But throughout Russian political history, all these political forms, which have qualitative differences and are founded on different and sometimes directly contradictory ideological principles, had a set of common traits. Everywhere, we see the political expression of the social arrangements characteristic of a society of the continental, "land-based," heroic type. These sociological peculiarities emerged in politics through the phe-

---

13 Werner Sombart (1863–1941) was a German economist and sociologist who was very much opposed to capitalism and democracy.—Ed.

14 Pitirim Sorokin (1889–1968) was a Russian sociologist who was a Social Revolutionary during the Russian Revolution, and was opposed to Communism. He left Russia and lived for the remainder of his life in the United States.—Ed.

15 Pitirim Sorokin, *Social and Cultural Dynamics* (Boston: Porter Sargent Publishers, 1970).

16 Peter I (1672–1725), or Peter the Great, was the first Czar to be called "Emperor of all Russia," and instituted many reforms which led to the development of the Russian Empire as it was later known.—Ed.

nomenon that the philosopher-Eurasianists of the 1920s[17] called "ideocracy." The ideational model in the sociocultural sphere, as a general trait of Russian society throughout its history, was expressed in politics as ideocracy, which also had different ideological forms, but preserved a vertical, hierarchical, "messianic" structure of government.

The Russian Federation and the Geopolitical Map of the World

After fixing the well-defined geopolitical identity of contemporary Russia, we can move to the next stage. Taking into account such a geopolitical analysis, we can precisely determine the place of the contemporary Russian Federation on the *geopolitical* map of the world.

The Russian Federation is in the Heartland. The historical structure of Russian society displays vividly expressed tellurocratic traits. Without hesitation, we should associate the Russian Federation, too, with a government of the land-based type, and contemporary Russian society with a mainly holistic society.

The consequences of this geopolitical identification are global in scale. On its basis, we can make a series of deductions, which must lie at the basis of a consistent and fully-fledged Russian geopolitics of the future.

1. Russia's geopolitical identity, being land-based and tellurocratic, demands strengthening, deepening, acknowledgement, and development. The substantial side of the policy of affirming political sovereignty, declared in the early 2000s by the President of the Russian Federation, Vladimir Putin, consists in precisely this. Russia's political sovereignty is imbued with a much deeper significance: it is the realization of the strategic project for the upkeep of the political-administrative unity of the Heartland and the (re)creation of the conditions

---

17 Among the Russian émigrés who were living in exile following the Revolution, the idea of Eurasianism was born, which held that Russia was a distinct civilization from that of Europe, and that the Revolution had been a necessary step in giving rise to a new Russia that would be freer of Western, modernizing influences.—Ed.

necessary for Russia to act as *the tellurocratic pole on a global scale*. In strengthening Russia's sovereignty, we strengthen one of the columns of the world's geopolitical architecture; we carry out an operation, much greater in scale than a project of domestic policy concerning only our immediate neighbors, in the best case. Geopolitically, *the fact that Russia is the Heartland makes its sovereignty a planetary problem*. All the powers and states in the world that possess tellurocratic properties depend on whether Russia will cope with this historic challenge and be able to preserve and strengthen its sovereignty.

2. Beyond any ideological preferences, Russia is doomed to conflict with the civilization of the Sea, with thalassocracy, embodied today in the USA and *the unipolar America-centric world order*. Geopolitical dualism has nothing in common with the ideological or economic peculiarities of this or that country. A global geopolitical conflict unfolded between the Russian Empire and the British monarchy, then between the socialist camp and the capitalist camp. Today, during the age of the democratic republican arrangement, the same conflict is unfolding between democratic Russia and the bloc of the democratic countries of NATO treading upon it. *Geopolitical regularities lie deeper than political-ideological contradictions or similarities.* The discovery of this principal conflict does not automatically mean war or a direct strategic conflict. Conflict can be understood in different ways. From the position of realism in international relations, we are talking about a conflict of interests which leads to war only when one of the sides is sufficiently convinced of the weakness of the other, or when an elite is put at the head of either state that puts national interests above rational calculation. The conflict can also develop peacefully, through a system of a general strategic, economic, technological, and diplomatic balance. Occasionally it can even soften into rivalry and competition, although a forceful resolution can never be consciously ruled out. In such a situation the question of *geopolitical security* is foremost, and without it

no other factors — modernization, an increase in the Gross Domestic Product (GDP) or the standard of living, and so forth — have independent significance. What is the point of our creating a developed economy if we will lose our geopolitical independence? This is not "bellicose," but a healthy rational analysis in a realist spirit; this is *geopolitical realism*.

3. Geopolitically, *Russia is something more than the Russian Federation in its current administrative borders.* The Eurasian civilization, established around the Heartland with its core in the Russian *narod*, is much broader than contemporary Russia. To some degree, practically all the countries of the Commonwealth of Independent States (CIS) belong to it. Onto this *sociological* peculiarity, a *strategic* factor is superimposed: to guarantee its territorial security, Russia must take military control over the center of the zones attached to it, in the south and the west, and in the sphere of the northern Arctic Ocean. Moreover, if we consider Russia — a planetary tellurocratic pole, then it becomes apparent that its direct interests extend throughout the Earth and touch all the continents, seas, and oceans. Hence, it becomes necessary to elaborate a *global geopolitical strategy* for Russia, describing in detail the specific interests relating to each country and each region.

CHAPTER II

The Geopolitics of the USSR

The Geopolitical Background of the 1917 Revolution

The end of the Czarist dynasty did not yet signify the end of the First World War for Russia. And although one of the reasons for the overthrow of the Romanovs was the difficulties of the war and the strain it put on human resources, the economy, and the whole social infrastructure of Russian society, the forces that came to power after the abdication of Nicholas II from the throne (the Provisional Government,[18] formed mainly on the

---

18 The Provisional Government arose in the aftermath of the abdication of Czar Nicholas II in March 1917, and was intended to organize the elections that would lead to the formation of a new government. It was made up of a coalition of many different parties. Following the Bolshevik revolution in October, it was abolished.—Ed.

basis of the Freemasonry of the Duma[19] and bourgeois parties) continued the course of Russia's participation in the war on the side of the Triple Entente.[20]

Geopolitically, this point is decisive. Both Nicholas II and the partisans of the republican, bourgeois-democratic form of government aligned with him were oriented toward England and France; they strove to position Russia in the camp of *thalassocratic* states. Domestically, there were irreconcilable contradictions between the monarchic model and the bourgeois-

---

19   However, the most populous lodge of the Great East of Russia's Peoples (a Masonic lodge in Czarist Russia—Ed.) in 1912–1916 was undoubtedly the Duma lodge, "the Rose," which the Masonic deputies of the Fourth State Duma joined in 1912. It was opened on November 15, 1912. Its principle difference from the Third Duma consisted in the explicit decrease of the center (the number of Octobrists in the Duma was sharply reduced: instead of 120, only 98 remained, while the number of Rightists grew to 185 from 148; and the number of Leftists, members of the Constitutional Democratic Party (known as Kadets—Ed.) and progressives increased from 98 to 107).

The demarcation of political forces in the Duma intensified, and with it the hopes of the government for the creation of a pro-government majority in it collapsed. From year to year, the Fourth State Duma became ever more opposed to the leadership, and what's more, criticism of it was heard not only on the Left but also on the Right.

The Octobrist M. V. Rodzianko became the chairman of the Fourth State Duma.

There were at least 23 Freemasons in the Fourth State Duma: V. A. Vinogradov, N. K. Volkov, I. P. Demidov, A. M. Kolyubakin, N. V. Nekrasov, A. A. Orlov-Davidov, V. A. Stepanov, F. F. Kokoshin, K. K. Chernosvitov, A. I. Shingarev, F. A. Golovin, D. N. Grigorovich-Barsky, N. P. Vasilenko, F. R. Steinheil, A. N. Bokeikhanov, A. A. Svechin, E. P. Gegechkori, M. I. Skobelev, N. C. Chkheidze, A. I. Chkhenkeli, I. N Efremov, A. I. Konovalov, and A. F. Kerensky. All of them, as has already been noted, were members of the Duma lodge, "the Rose." The progressive, I. N. Efremov, directed it.

The decisive condition for admission into the Duma lodge was not the deputy's party affiliation, as is customary in Duma factions, but precisely his organizational affiliation to one of the Masonic lodges.

"In the Fourth State Duma," testified former Freemason L. A. Velikhov, "I entered the so-called Masonic association, into which entered the representatives from the Leftist progressives (Efremov), the Leftist Kadets (Nekrasov, Volkov, Stepanov), the *trudoviks* (Kerensky), Social Democrats (Chkheidze, Skobelev) and which set as its aim a bloc of all the Duma's opposition parties for the overthrow of the autocracy." From the Kadets, besides the aforementioned L. A. Velikhov, Volkov, Nekrasov and Stepanov, V. A. Vinogradov, I. P. Demidov, A. M. Kolyubakin, A. A. Orlov-Davidov and V. A. Stepanov also entered. From the Mensheviks, E. P. Gegechkori, M. I. Skobelev, N. C. Chkheidze, A. I. Chkhenkeli; from the progressives, I. N. Efremov and A. I. Konovalov; and from the *trudoviks*, A. F. Kerensky.

Aleksei Serkov, *The History of Russian Freemasonry 1845–1945* (Saint Petersburg: Novikoff Publishing, 2000).

20   The Triple Entente was an alliance between the United Kingdom, France, and Russia that was established in 1907.—Ed.

democratic one, and the escalation of these contradictions led to the over-throw of the dynasty and the monarchy. But in the geopolitical orientation of Nicholas II and the Provisional leadership there was, on the contrary, *continuity and succession* — an orientation toward the civilization of the Sea created an affinity between them. For the Czar this was a practical choice and for the "Februarists,"[21] an ideological one, since England and France were long-established bourgeois regimes.

On February 25, 1917, by a royal decree, the activity of the Fourth State Duma was suspended. On the evening of February 27, a Provisional Committee of the State Duma was created whose Chairman was M. V. Rodzyanko (an Octobrist, and Chairman of the Fourth Duma). The Committee took upon itself the functions and authority of the supreme power. On March 2, 1917, Emperor Nicholas II abdicated, and transferred the right of inheritance to the Grand Duke Michael Alexandrovich,[22] who, in turn, declared his intention on March 3 to adopt supreme authority only after the will of the people expressed itself in the Constituent Assembly about the final form that the government was to take.

On March 2, 1917 the Provisional Committee of the State Duma formed the first public offices. The new leadership announced elections in the Constituent Assembly, and a democratic law concerning elections was adopted; there would be universal, equal, direct, and secret ballots. The old government organs were abolished. At the head of the Provisional Committee was the Chairman of the Soviet of Ministers and the Minister of Internal Affairs, Prince G. E. Lvov (former member of the First State Duma and Chairman of the Main Committee of the All-Russian Zemsky Union). Meanwhile, the Soviet, whose task was to oversee the actions of

---

21 Those who supported the Provisional Government that was established following the February Revolution of 1917.—Ed.

22 Michael Alexandrovich (1878–1918) was a prince who was second in line to the throne of the Czar. Following the abdication of Nicholas II, Alexandrovich was selected to succeed him over the Czar's own son, Alexei, as the latter was regarded as being too ill to rule. He refused to accept the throne, however. This did not win him any favors from the Bolsheviks, who murdered him in 1918.—Ed.

the Provisional Government, continued to function. As a consequence, dual power was established in Russia. The Soviets of Workers and Soldiers' Deputies[23] were controlled by Left-wing parties, which previously remained largely outside the State Duma: Socialist Revolutionaries[24] and social democrats[25] (Mensheviks[26] and Bolsheviks). In foreign policy, the Bolsheviks, led by. Lenin and Trotsky, successively followed a *pro-German orientation.* This pro-German orientation was based on a few factors: close cooperation between Bolsheviks and German Marxist Social Democrats, and secret agreements with the Kaiser's intelligence agency about material and technical assistance given to the Bolsheviks. Moreover, the Bolsheviks relied on the disapproval of the war by the broad masses. They based their propaganda on this, formulating it in the spirit of revolutionary ideology: the solidarity of the working classes of all countries and the imperial character of war itself, which opposed the interests of the masses. Hence, the dual power divided between the Provisional Government and the Soviets (who were under the control of the Bolsheviks from the beginning) in the interval between March and October 1917 reflected two geopolitical vectors, the pro-English and pro-French one for the Provisional Government, and the pro-German one for the Bolsheviks. This duality also reveals its significance and its character in those historical events that are directly connected with the epoch of the Revolution and the Civil War.

On April 18, 1917, the first governmental crisis broke out, ending with the formation of the first coalition government on May 5, 1917, with the

---

23 These councils were established following the February Revolution to maintain order until elections could be held, and to determine the nature and composition of the new government.—Ed.

24 The Socialist Revolutionaries were socialists, but not Marxists. They were one of the major parties in Russia at the time of the Revolution.—Ed.

25 Both the Bolsheviks and the Mensheviks were offshoots of the Russian Social Democratic Labor Party. Following the departure of the Mensheviks, it became a Bolshevik organization, eventually becoming the Communist Party of the USSR.—Ed.

26 The Mensheviks had undergone a split with the Bolsheviks in 1904 over matters of ideology and membership in the Party. Thereafter they were a Communist opposition party, viewed as having been more moderate than the Bolsheviks.—Ed.

participation of the socialists. Its cause was P. N. Milyukov's[27] April 18 note addressed to England and France, in which he announced that the Provisional Government would continue the war to its triumphant end and continue all the international agreements that had been made by the Czarist government. Here we are dealing with a geopolitical choice that influenced domestic processes. The decision of the Provisional Government led to popular indignation, which spilled over into mass meetings and demonstrations, with demands for a quick end to the war, the resignation of P. N. Milyukov and A. I. Guchkov,[28] and the transfer of power to the Soviets. These disturbances were organized by the Bolsheviks and the Socialist Revolutionaries. P. N. Milyukov and A. I. Guchkov left the government. On May 5, an agreement was reached between the Provisional Government and the Executive Committee of the Petrograd Soviet for the creation of a coalition. However, the extreme Left parties were not unified around a geopolitical policy. The Bolsheviks held more logically to a pro-German and anti-war line. A part of the Mensheviks and the Leftist Socialist Revolutionaries (whose leaders also often belonged to Masonic organizations, where a pro-French and pro-English orientation dominated) were inclined to support the Provisional Government, in which the Socialist Revolutionaries had by then received a few posts.

The first All-Russian Congress of Soviets of Workers and Soldiers' Deputies, which took place during June 3–24, was dominated by the Socialist Revolutionaries and the Mensheviks, leading them to support the Provisional Government and to reject the demand of the Bolsheviks to end the war and transfer power to the Soviets. Then the quick collapse of Russia began. On June 3 a delegation from the Provisional Government, led by ministers Tereshchenko and Tsereteli, recognized the autonomy of the

---

27 Pavel Milyukov (1859–1943) was the Minister of Foreign Affairs in the Provisional Government.—Ed.

28 Alexander Guchkov (1862–1936) was the Minister of War in the Provisional Government.—Ed.

Ukrainian Central Rada (UCR).[29] Meanwhile, without the approval of the government, a delegation outlined the geographical limits of the authority of the UCR, including some of the southwestern provinces of Russia. This provoked the July crisis.[30] At the height of the July crisis the Finnish Seim[31] proclaimed the independence of Finland from Russia in its domestic affairs and limited the competence of the Provisional Government to questions of war and foreign policy. Because of the crisis, a second coalition government was formed with the Social Revolutionary A. F. Kerensky in charge. Socialist Revolutionaries and Mensheviks occupied a total of seven posts in this government.

The Social Revolutionary Kerensky, who was also in the group of *Trudoviks* (*narodi* socialists), was a prominent figure in the Russian Freemasonry of the Duma, a member of the "Little Bear" lodge, and a secretary of the secret congregative Masonic organization, "The Supreme Soviet of the Great East of the Peoples of Russia." Kerensky held to a pro-English orientation and was closely connected to English Freemasonry. On September 1, 1917, with the goal of opposing the Petrograd Soviet, Kerensky formed a new organ of power, the Directory (Soviet of Five), which proclaimed Russia a republic and dissolved the Fourth State Duma. On September 14, 1917, the All-Russian Democratic Conference was opened, which had to decide the question of the ruling authority, with the participation of all political parties. The Bolsheviks left it in protest. On September 25, 1917, Kerensky formed the third coalition government. On the night of October 26, 1917, on behalf of the Soviets, the Bolsheviks, anarchists, and Leftist Socialist Revolutionaries overthrew the Provisional

---

29 The UCR was the council that assumed power in Ukraine following the February Revolution in Russia with the intention of securing Ukrainian independence. It was declared illegal by the Soviets in December 1917.—Ed.

30 Between July 3 and 7, soldiers and workers in Petrograd, backed by the Bolsheviks, held demonstrations against the Provisional Government. The government, accusing the demonstrators of fomenting a coup and suppressed it using military force, leading to a temporary setback for the Bolsheviks.—Ed.

31 The Seim was the Finnish popular assembly.—Ed.

Government and arrested its members. Kerensky fled. Significantly, he was helped by English diplomats, in particular Bruce Lockhart,[32] and was sent to England, where, from his very arrival, he was active in English Masonic lodges. Geopolitically, the October Bolshevik revolution, which different historical schools and representatives of various worldviews evaluate in different ways today, was special because it signified *an abrupt change in the orientation of Russia's foreign policy from a thalassocratic to a tellurocratic one.* Nicholas II and the Masonic-republicans of the Duma from the Provisional Government had held an Anglo-French orientation and were faithful to the Entente. The Bolsheviks were unequivocally oriented toward peace with Germany and departure from the Entente.

After the disbandment of the Constituent Assembly,[33] where the Bolsheviks did not receive the support necessary to fully legalize their seizure of authority, authority was transferred to the Council of Peoples' Commissars, where the Bolsheviks dominated. Then, the Leftist Socialist Revolutionaries were their allies.

On March 3, 1918, a separate peace agreement between the Bolsheviks and representatives of the Central Powers (Germany, Austro-Hungary, Turkey, and Bulgaria) was concluded at Brest-Litovsk, signifying Russia's exit from the First World War. According to the terms of the agreement, the Privislinskie provinces, Ukraine, those provinces with a primarily Belorussian population, the Province of Estonia, the Province of Courland, the Province of Livonia, the Grand Principality of Finland, the Kars dis-

---

32 Sir Robert Hamilton Bruce Lockhart (1887–1970) was the British Consul-General at the time of the Russian Revolution. On behalf of his superiors in London, and in conjunction with the Secret Intelligence Service, he attempted to persuade the Bolsheviks to remain in the war against Germany, but was unsuccessful. After a series of covert attempts to influence the course of the Revolution, in 1918, with the secret agent Sidney Reilly, he attempted to have Lenin assassinated and the Bolsheviks overthrown, becoming known as the "Lockhart Plot." It failed, although Lockhart was later allowed to leave Russia in a prisoner exchange.—Ed.

33 The All Russian Constituent Assembly was formed as the result of an election held in November 1917. When it became clear that the number of representatives from the Socialist Revolutionaries would outnumber the Bolsheviks in the Assembly by a wide margin, they began casting doubt on the validity of the Assembly, and it was only allowed to meet for one session in January 1918 before it was dissolved.—Ed.

trict, and the Batumsk district on the Caucasus were all torn away from Russia's West. The Soviet leadership promised to halt the war with the Ukrainian Central Soviet (Rada) of the Ukrainian People's Republic, to demobilize the army and fleet, to remove the Baltic fleet from its bases in Finland and the Baltic states, to transfer the Black Sea fleet with all its infrastructure to the central states, and to pay out six million marks in reparations. A territory of 780,000 square kilometers, comprising a population of 56 million people (a third of the population of the Russian Empire), was seized from Soviet Russia. At the same time, Russia brought all its troops out of the designated areas, while Germany, on the other hand, brought its troops in and retained control over the Monzundski Archipelago and the Gulf of Riga.

Such was the enormous price that Soviet Russia (in part because it expected an imminent proletarian revolution in Germany and other European countries) paid for its pro-German orientation.

The Brest treaty was immediately rejected by the Leftist Socialist Revolutionaries, a part of whose leadership was oriented toward France and England from former times. As a sign of protest against the conditions of the armistice, the Leftist Socialist Revolutionaries left the Council of Peoples' Commissars; at the Fourth Congress of Soviets, they voted against the Brest treaty. The Social Revolutionary S. D. Mstislavskii coined the slogan, "No war, so an uprising!" urging the "masses" to "rise up" against the German-Austrian occupying forces. On July 5, at the Fifth Congress of Soviets, the Leftist Socialist Revolutionaries again actively came out against the Bolsheviks' policies, condemning the Brest treaty. On July 6, the day after the opening of the Congress, two Leftist Socialist Revolutionaries, Yakov

Blumkin[34] and Nikolai Andreev, officials of the All-Russian Extraordinary Committee (AEC), entered the German embassy in Moscow following a mandate from the AEC, and Andreev shot and killed the German ambassador, Mirbach. The goal of the Socialist Revolutionaries was to wreck the agreements with Germany. On July 30, the Leftist Social Revolutionary, B. M. Donskoi, liquidated the general in command of the occupying forces, Eichhorn, in Kiev. The leader of the Leftist Socialist Revolutionaries, Maria Spiridonova, was sent to the Fifth Congress of Soviets, where she announced that "the Russian people are free from Mirbach," implying that the pro-German line in Soviet Russia was finished. In response, the Bolsheviks mobilized their forces for the suppression of the "Leftist Social Revolutionary uprising," and arrested and executed their leaders. In this there again appeared a distinction in geopolitical orientations: this time, among the radical Leftist forces that had seized power in Soviet Russia. The Leftist Socialist Revolutionaries had tried to wreck the pro-German line of the Bolsheviks, but they failed and promptly disappeared as a political force.

If we gather all these geopolitical elements together, we get the following picture: Nicholas II, the bourgeois parties and, in part, the Leftist Socialist Revolutionaries (the Freemasons of the Duma) maintained an orientation toward the Entente, and, as a result, toward thalassocracy; while the Bolsheviks consistently pursued a policy of cooperation with Germany and other Central European states, and with Turkey; that is, they came out in favor of tellurocracy. This geopolitical pattern allows us to take a new look at the dramatic events of Russia's history during 1917–1918 and predetermines the developments of the Soviet period.

---

34 Yakov Blumkin (1898–1929) was the head of the Cheka's (the revolutionary secret police) counter-intelligence operations at the time. He was forgiven by the Bolsheviks for having participated I the SR coup, and later worked as an assassin and a secret agent. Dispatched to help foment revolutionary subversion against the British in the Middle East, his Oriental adventures made him famous. He later befriended Trotsky, After Trotsky's exile from the USSR, he acted as a courier for Trotsky's messages; when this was discovered, he was executed on Stalin's orders.—Ed.

The Geopolitics of the Civil War

The Civil War broke out in Russia between 1917 and 1923. We will consider its geopolitical aspects. Although the Civil War was a domestic conflict, in which the citizens of a single government fought, geopolitics and competing ties with foreign powers played a considerable role in it. What we know about the players' geopolitical orientations in the final years of the Czar's regime and after February and October 1917 already allows us to give a preliminary characterization of the geopolitical processes of the Civil War.

In the Civil War, mainly two political parties fought: the Reds (Bolsheviks) and the Whites.[35] As for the Bolsheviks, their ideological, political, and geopolitical identity was clear. They professed Marxism and the dictatorship of the proletariat, came out against the bourgeois order of things, and were geopolitically oriented toward Germany and rigidly opposed to the Entente. From this we immediately see a few tellurocratic traits:

- orientation toward Germany (the Brest-Litovsk treaty);
- rejection of the bourgeois order (capitalism, as we saw, is sociologically associated with thalassocracy);
- hostility toward the thalassocratic Entente.

We can also say that the Bolsheviks cultivated a "Spartan" style: asceticism, heroism, and devotion to an idea.

The White movement was not as uniform, ideologically or politically. Both those who continued the "February" trend (the overwhelming majority) and those who supported a return to the monarchy participated in it. Moreover, among the supporters of the February Revolution were repre-

---

35 The White movement was a coalition of anti-Bolshevik forces, including monarchists, socialists, conservatives, democrats and others who wanted to overthrow the Bolsheviks. It received support from the émigrés and from Western governments. The movement was named after the color of the uniforms of the Czarist army.—Ed.

sentatives of various parties, both Right and bourgeois parties (Kadets,[36] Octobrists)[37] and Leftists (Socialist Revolutionaries, people's socialists, etc.). Ideologically, the White movement represented many forces, whose political ideas were diverse. Only one thing united them: a rejection of Bolshevism and Marxism. The Reds served as a "common enemy." But as the Bolsheviks in that historical situation represented *tellurocracy*, it is perfectly logical that their adversaries, the Whites, would be oriented in the opposite direction, toward *thalassocracy*. It happened this way in practice, too, because the White movement as a whole bet on the Entente and on the support of England and France in the struggle against the Bolsheviks. This was part of the logic of the Provisional Government's foreign policy and the policies of the monarchists, who maintained faithfulness to their allies according to the logic of the final stage of Czarist rule.

Only a few, small segments of the White movement (in particular the Cossack Ataman[38] Krasnov, and the "northern army," which had been created by the Germans in October 1918 in Pskov and consisted of Russian volunteers) maintained a German orientation, but this was a completely marginal phenomenon.

Moreover, if we look at a map of the location of the main territories controlled by the Reds and Whites during the Civil War, we notice the following pattern: the Reds controlled the inner-continental zones, the space of the Heartland, while the White armies were arranged along Russia's periphery, and in varying degrees in the coastal zones from which came the help of the sea powers and that supported the White cause politically, economically, militarily, and strategically. In this, too, the Whites followed the logic of thalassocracy, which considers political and strategic processes

---

36 The Kadets were the members of the Constitutional Democratic Party, which favored democratic reforms and a constitutional monarchy.—Ed.

37 The Octobrists, or the Union of October 17, was a centrist party that supported constitutional monarchy in Russia in accordance with Nicholas II's October Manifesto, issued in the aftermath of the Revolution of 1905.—Ed.

38 A Cossack leader.—Ed.

from a coastal perspective. The Reds were in the position of land-based geo-political powers.

In the era of the Civil War, we see a phenomenon that is highly symbolic and important for geopolitics. In 1919, the founding father of geopolitics, Halford Mackinder, was appointed British High Commissioner for southern Russia and was sent through Eastern Europe to support the anti-Bolshevist forces led by General Denikin. This mission allowed Mackinder to give his recommendations about geopolitics in Eastern Europe to the British government, which laid the foundations for his book, *Democratic Ideals and Reality*. Mackinder called on Great Britain to strengthen its support for the White armies in the south of Russia and to involve the anti-Bolshevist and anti-Russian regimes of Poland, Bulgaria, and Romania for this purpose. In his negotiations with Denikin, they were in agreement about the separation from Russia of the southern and western regions and the South Caucasus, for the creation of a pro-English buffer state. Mackinder's analysis of the state of affairs in Russia during the Civil War was absolutely unequivocal: he saw in the Bolsheviks the forces of the Heartland, destined either to bear a Communist ideological form or to cede the initiative to Germany. England could allow neither. So Mackinder offered to support the Whites however he could and to dismember Russia. It is important to note what countries he tried to establish under the purview of a nominally integral (for that period) government: Belarus, Ukraine, Yugorussia (under the primary influence of pro-British Poland), Dagestan (including the entire North Caucasus), Armenia, Azerbaijan, and Georgia. These countries were to be a *cordon sanitaire*[39] between continental Russia and its neighboring regions, Germany in the west, and Turkey and Iran in the south. Mackinder's book *Democratic Ideals and Reality* and his note[40] to his friend

---

39 French: "quarantine line," applied to the newly-independent states between the USSR and Europe in the hope that they could serve as a bulwark against the spread of Communism.—Ed.

40 Brian Blouet, "Sir Halford Mackinder as British High Commissioner to South Russia 1919–1920," *Geographical Journal* 142 (1976), pp. 228–236.

Lord Curzon[41] contain the basic ideas of geopolitics, which Mackinder not only created and developed theoretically, but also practiced.

The situation on the southern front in 1920 and the weakened armies of Denikin caused Mackinder's plan, which he voiced at a meeting of the British government on January 29, 1920, not to be adopted; England refused to give the Whites full support.[42] But Mackinder's analysis of the general situation, then hardly evident, proved its brilliance over time. Most English politicians were convinced that the Bolshevik regime would not last long. Mackinder, on the other hand, using the geopolitical method, clearly foresaw that Soviet Russia would eventually transform into a powerful continental tellurocratic state. And this is how it later turned out.

The participation in the White movement of a figure like Mackinder, the founder of geopolitics and the leading figure of the thalassocratic strategy, definitively confirms the thalassocratic nature of the Whites on the whole.

No less significant is the fate of another figure, Aleksei Efimovich Vandam (Edrikhin), an outstanding analyst of international relations, and a strategist who can be easily ranked among the heralds of Russian Eurasian continental geopolitics. During the Civil War, Edrikhin was in Estonia, which was occupied by the Germans. The German General Staff commissioned him to form a "Northern Army," consisting of anti-Bolshevist forces loyal to the Germans. Vandam is famous for his rigid anti-English and tellurocratic positions (he participated in military actions in South Africa against the English on the side of the Boers), and precisely this factor became decisive for the Germans. The "Northern Army" did not develop, because of Germany's defeat in the First World War, and Vandam's mission did not continue. But the fact that this project involved the participation of an eminent Russian geopolitician is exceedingly symbolic.

---

41 George Curzon (1859–1925) was a British politician particularly concerned about countering the influence of Russia in Central Asia. He served as Viceroy of colonial India, and was Foreign Secretary at the time that Mackinder was in Russia.—Ed.

42 Ibid.

In the Civil War, among figures of secondary importance, we meet another individual whose fate was important for the establishment of geopolitics, Peter Nikolaevich Savitskii. In 1919, Savitskii joined the volunteer movement of south Russia ("the Denikins") and was a "comrade" of the Minister of Foreign Relations in the government of Denikin and Wrangel. In 1919, at the height of the Civil War, Savitskii wrote a geopolitical text, astonishing in its sagacity, entitled *Outlines of International Relations*,[43] where he announced the following: "One can say with certainty that if the Soviet government had overpowered Kolchak[44] and Denikin, it would have 'reunited' the entire space of the former Russian Empire and would very likely have passed beyond its former borders in its conquests."[45] The article was printed in one of the periodicals of the Whites and in the person of one of the theoreticians of their international politics. Savitskii shows unambiguously that the Whites and the Reds have the same geopolitical goals: the establishment of a powerful continental state, independent from the West, for which both will be compelled to carry out an essentially identical policy. Later, Savitskii became the main figure of the Eurasianist movement, which imparted to the intuitions of the continuity of the geopolitical strategy of land-based states a developed theoretical foundation, becoming the core of the first full-blown Russian geopolitical school.[46]

In the Civil War, three stages can be distinguished: the first is from 1917 through November 1918, when the basic military camps, the Reds and Whites, were formed. This unfolded against the background of the First World War. The second stage is from November 1918 through March 1920, when the main battle between the Red Army and the White armies occurred. In March 1920, a radical shift in the Civil War set in. In this period,

---

43 Petr Savitskii, *Outlines of International Relations* (Krasnodar, 1919); *The Continent Eurasia* (Moscow: Agraf, 1997), pp. 382–398.

44 Admiral Aleksandr Kolchak (1874–1920) was appointed as Supreme Commander of the White forces in 1918, a position he held until his execution by the Bolsheviks in 1920.—Ed.

45 Ibid., p. 390.

46 Alexander Dugin, *Foundations of Geopolitics* (Moscow: Arctogaia, 2000).

an abrupt decrease of military actions from the side of the forces of the
Entente occurred, due to the end of the First World War and the withdraw-
al of the main contingent of foreign troops from the territory of Russia.
After this, it was chiefly Russians in combat operations. Fighting was then
widespread in Russia. At first, the advance of the Whites was successful,
but the initiative passed to the Reds, who took control of the principal territory of the country.

From March 1920 through October 1922, the third stage occurred,
in which the primary struggle was on the outskirts of the country and no
longer constituted an immediate threat to the authority of the Bolsheviks.
After the evacuation in October 1922 of the Far-Eastern Zemskaya Rat'
of General Diterikhs, the struggle was continued only by the Siberian
Volunteer Armed Force of Lieutenant General A. N. Pepelyaev, which had
fought in the Yakutsk region until June 1923, and the Cossack squadron
of Army Sergeant Bologov, which had remained near Nikolsk-Ussuriisk.
Soviet authority was finally established in Kamchatka and Chukchi in
1923. It is significant that all the military actions took place according to
the scheme of *the Red center* (Heartland) against *the White periphery* along
the borders of the sea, and that the remnants of the defeated White troops
left Russia by sea.

The outcome of the Civil War was the seizure of power by the Bolsheviks
over most of the territory of the former Russian Empire; the recognition
of the independence of Poland, Lithuania, Latvia, Estonia and Finland;
and the creation of the Soviet Union in the territories of the Russian,
Ukrainian, Belorussian, and trans-Caucasian republics under their control,
through an agreement signed on December 30, 1922. Savitskii's predic-
tion about Ukraine, Belarus, and the South Caucasus proved accurate: the
Bolsheviks did not grant these territories independence, but included them
in the composition of the Soviet state.

It is revealing that in their Caucasian policy, the Reds relied on Kemal
Atatürk's Turkey, carrying out precisely a *continental* geopolitics on this

issue. The eminent military and diplomatic actor, who crossed to the side of Bolsheviks, General S. I. Aralov,[47] the founder of the Glavnoye Razvedyvatel'noye Upravleniye (GRU),[48] played a major role in this approach to Turkey and in the reorganization of the strategic balance of powers in the Caucasus.

The Geopolitical Balance of Power in the Peace of Versailles

The end of the First World War produced a new balance of powers. Russia lost to Germany and Austro-Hungary, and this loss was fixed by the conditions of the Brest-Litovsk treaty. The costs of this treaty were significant. But as the Bolsheviks had a pro-German orientation, Russia could not exploit the fact that Germany, in turn, lost to France and England. As a result, on June 28, 1919, a peace treaty was signed in the Palace of Versailles by the United States, Great Britain, France, Italy, and Japan on the one side, and Germany on the other, establishing the international order for the next decade.

The Treaty of Versailles was humiliating for Germany, essentially depriving it of the right to conduct an independent policy, to have a fully-fledged army, to develop its economy, and to reestablish its influence on the international stage. Moreover, demands were made on Germany to make significant and extremely painful territorial concessions. The geopolitics of the Versailles peace focused on the global interests of the sea states, primarily the British Empire. Essentially, England was recognized almost *de jure* as the sole legal owner of the world's oceans. This was a triumph of thalassocracy. Bolshevik Russia was factored out altogether, and defeated Germany was put in onerous fetters. It is revealing that Halford Mackinder, who, as we already said, was closely associated with the English Minister of Foreign Affairs, Lord Curzon, influenced the architecture of the Versailles

---

47 Semyon Aralov, *Memoirs of a Soviet Diplomat 1922–1923* (Moscow: Institute of International Relations,1960).

48 The military intelligence arm of the Red Army.—Ed.

treaty. The main task, according to Mackinder, was to prevent the rise of Bolshevist Russia and Germany and especially to foreclose any future strategic alliance between them. There was a plan to construct a *cordon sanitaire* out of existing or newly established Eastern European governments oriented toward England and France that was expected to control and limit potential Russian-German relations.

The Versailles world was a world of victorious thalassocracy, the grandiose political and military success of the civilization of the Sea. We should especially underscore that the American delegation to the Versailles conference, under the leadership of President Woodrow Wilson, first voiced the new international strategy of the USA, in which it was asserted that the whole world was the zone of American interests and in which, essentially, the idea of overtaking England's initiative as the bastion of sea power was secured. That is, Admiral Mahan's[49] ideas became the basis for the USA's strategic course during the twentieth century, the course it still follows today. The Wilson Doctrine called for an end to American isolationism and non-interference in the affairs of European states, and for the switch to an active policy on a planetary scale under the aegis of the sea-based civilization. From this moment, the gradual transfer of the center of gravity from Britain to the USA began.

This point may be considered the turning point in the geopolitical course of North America: from now on, the USA stood firmly on the path of a consistent and active thalassocracy and perceived its social structure (bourgeois democracy, the market society, liberal ideology) as a universal set of global values and as the ideology and foundation of a planetary hegemony. In the period between the Treaty of Versailles and the beginning of the Second World War, the shift of the center from England to the USA

---

49 Alfred Mahan (1840–1914), in his strategic writings, emphasized sea power above all else in military matters, and called for the modernization of the American Navy. His ideas were very influential, both at home and in Europe.—Ed.

would be the principal geopolitical process, proceeding in the context of the civilization of the Sea.

It is at Versailles, at the prompting of a group of American experts and big bankers who attended from the USA, that the Council on Foreign Relations (CFR) was formed under the leadership of the American geopolitician Isaiah Bowman,[50] destined to become the most important authority in the formation of American foreign policy on a global scale in the thalassocratic spirit. The systematic establishment of a school of American geopolitics began precisely at this crucial moment. At the same time, Halford Mackinder, who was present in the British delegation at the conclusion of the Versailles Treaty, also began to cooperate with the CFR. Later, Mackinder would publish his works on policy in an influential journal published by the CFR, *Foreign Affairs*. Thus the foundation was laid for a systematized *geopolitical Atlanticism*, based on the strategic unity of the two great Anglo-Saxon states, England and the USA. And if the USA played a subordinate role at Versailles, then the balance of power would slowly shift in its favor, and the USA would gradually come to the forefront, taking upon itself the function of the bulwark of the whole marine civilization, and becoming the core of sea power and a global oceanic thalassocratic empire.

The history of German geopolitics, connected with the name and school of Karl Haushofer, also began at Versailles.[51] Haushofer provided an analysis of the results of the Treaty of Versailles in the spirit of Mackinder's method, but from the defeated German side. Thus, he came to a geopolitical description of a model that should have, at least theoretically, led Germany

---

50 Isaiah Bowman (1878–1950) was an advisor to Woodrow Wilson at Versailles, and was later a territorial advisor to the U.S. Department of State during the Second World War.—Ed.

51 Karl Haushofer (1869–1946) was a German General who helped to establish geopolitics as a discipline in Germany. A friend of Rudolf Hess, His ideas were influential on the development of the international strategy of the Nazis, although he himself was never a supporter of the Nazis, his wife being half-Jewish, and Haushofer himself was imprisoned at the Dachau concentration camp following the assassination attempt against Hitler in 1944, and his son was executed.—Ed.

to a future rebirth and to overcome the onerous conditions of Versailles. For this, Haushofer advanced the idea of a "continental bloc,"[52] representing an alliance of objectively land-based, continental, tellurocratic states: Germany, Russia, and Japan. Thus, a systematic and developed framework of continental geopolitics was assembled, representing a consistent and large-scale response to the strategy of the Atlanticists and geopoliticians of the thalassocratic school.

The trauma left by Versailles in German society would later be successfully exploited by the National Socialists (with whom Haushofer himself collaborated at first). Ultimately, it was precisely the plan of overcoming the constraints of Versailles that became one of the most important factors in the eventual Nazi victory in the Reichstag elections of 1933.

The Eurasian movement was formed by Russian émigrés in France after Versailles. It became the source of the foundations of Russian (Eurasian) geopolitics.[53]

The Geopolitics and Sociology of the Early Stalin Period

In 1922, Russia received a new name, becoming the Union of Soviet Socialist Republics. If, at first, the Bolsheviks related neutrally to the demands of the lesser peoples of the Russian Empire for independence and the creation of their own statehood, then a centralist tendency prevailed in the 1920s, called "Stalin's National Policy." The course was gradually taken to establish socialism in one country, which demanded strengthening Soviet power over the broadest space. For that reason, the Bolsheviks essentially returned to the Czarist policy of a centripetal orientation and the reinforcement of Russia's administrative unity. This time, however, this policy was formulated in entirely new ideological constructs and was founded

---

52 Karl Haushofer, *Der Kontinentalblock: Mitteleurope, Eurasien, Japan* (Berlin: Eher, 1941); Alexander Dugin, *The Foundations of Geopolitics* (Moscow: Arctogaia, 2000), pp. 825–836.

53 Petr Savitskii, "The Geographical and Geopolitical Foundations of Eurasianism," in *Twentieth-Century Classics of Geopolitics* (Moscow: AST Publishing, 2003); Petr Savitskii, *The Continent Eurasia* (Moscow: Agraf, 1997), pp. 295–303.

on proletarian internationalism, the equality of all peoples, and the class solidarity of all the proletarians of all nationalities. But its geopolitical essence remained as before: the Bolsheviks gathered the lands of the former Russian Empire *around the Heartland as a geopolitical core.* Sociologically, this unification proceeded under anti-bourgeois and "Spartan" slogans and on the basis of a new value system. This course started to diverge gradually from orthodox Marxism, which had imagined the proletarian revolution occurring, first, in industrially developed countries, and not in agrarian Russia (Marx himself categorically excluded this possibility); and, second, in many places at once or over a short time, not only in one country. Lenin and Trotsky, the major actors of the October Revolution and of the later Bolshevik retention of power, thought that the revolution could and must be in one country, which was already a certain deviation from classical Marxism. However, they interpreted this as a temporary historical peculiarity, after which a series of proletarian revolutions in different countries must follow, first in Germany, then also in England, France, and elsewhere. The Bolsheviks saw their moment as a transitional one, with the implementation of a proletarian revolution in one country as the first step in a whole series of revolutions in other countries, the start of a global process of world revolution. This is why the Bolsheviks agreed so readily to the harsh terms of the Germans at Brest-Litovsk: it was important for them to secure their position and hold out until the beginning of the revolution in the European states, which they thought was a matter both certain and imminent. Thus, Trotsky carried out active Marxist agitation, even attending Brest during the conclusion of the peace agreement.

Stalin himself, even in May 1924, wrote in his pamphlet *On the Foundations of Leninism,* "To overthrow the rule of the bourgeois and to install the rule of the proletariat in one country does not yet mean to secure the full victory of socialism. The main task of socialism, the organization of socialist production, still remains ahead. Can we resolve this task? Can we achieve the ultimate victory of socialism in one country without the combined efforts of the proletariat of a few advanced countries? No, it is not possible. For the ultimate victory of socialism, for the organization of socialist production, the efforts of one country, especially such a peasant country as Russia, is now not enough; for this the efforts of the proletariat of a few advanced countries is necessary."[54] Trotsky also continued to reason in this spirit.

But everything changed at the end of 1924, when the first contradictions between Trotsky and Stalin are to be found. Stalin completely denied his own words, despite having written them recently, and advanced a directly contradictory thesis. In December 1924, in one of his first works, *The October Revolution and the Tactics of the Russian Communists*,[55] a criticism of "Trotskyism," he asserted that "socialism can be built in one country." From this time he began to accuse those who denied the possibility of building socialism in the USSR without triumphant socialist revolutions in other countries of capitulation and defeatism. The new theoretical and political attitude towards building socialism in one country was secured at the Fourteenth Congress of the Russian Communist Party (of Bolsheviks) in December 1925. Later on "the building of socialism in one country" became an axiom of Soviet policy.

After this, hopes for proletarian revolution in other countries receded to a place of secondary importance, while the strategic tasks of securing the USSR as an independent great power capable of repelling an attack by the capitalists encircling them was moved to the forefront. With regard to the specifics of the geopolitical situation of the USSR in the Heartland and the sociological peculiarity of the "Spartan" style of socialist society, we are then dealing with a finished and full-fledged *tellurocracy*. Soviet Russia

---

54 Joseph Stalin, *On the Foundations of Leninism*, in Joseph Stalin, *Essays*, vol. 6 (Moscow: State Publisher of Political Literature, 1948). English translation: *Foundations of Leninism* (New York: International Publishers, 1939).

55 Joseph Stalin, 'The October Revolution and the Tactics of the Russian Communists,' in Joseph Stalin, *Essays*, vol. 6. English translation: *Problems of Leninism* (Peking: Foreign Languages Press, 1976).

in the Stalin period represents a new version of the great Turanic Eurasian empire,[56] the core of the land-based civilization.

Here we can raise the question: what is responsible for this change to a land-based Eurasian approach during the Soviet period of history: the content of Communist ideology, or the historical fact that the proletarian revolution occurred in land-based continental Russia? There is no unequivocal answer. Trotsky, even while he was still in the USSR and with yet greater persistence after his emigration, advanced the idea that Stalin's state "betrayed Communism" and recreated an imperial and great-power bureaucracy of the Czarist type on a new stage. Thereby, Trotsky tore socialism away from its Eurasian context and ascribed the peculiarities of the USSR (which he criticized) to a return to a national Russian strategy. A different point of view characterizes some contemporary Marxists (for instance, Costanzo Preve)[57] who see an internal connection between socialism and continentalism (the civilization of Land) and thereby consider the victory of socialism in land-based Russia (and later in other land-based, traditional societies: China, Vietnam, Korea, and so on) not an accident, but a regularity.

In any case, the construction of the USSR after 1924 shows how precise and true were the predictions of Mackinder and Savitskii, who considered from different points of view the geopolitical future of the Bolsheviks: the USSR became a powerful expression of the Heartland, while its confrontation with the capitalist world was a manifestation of the most important and perhaps even culminating phase of the "great war of continents," the battle between the land-based Behemoth and the sea-based Leviathan (in

---

56 The term Turanic refers to those peoples of Central Asia who were united by the Uraltaic group of languages. The Avars, who were a Turanic group of nomadic warriors, established a sizeable empire that spanned large areas of Central Asia and Eastern Europe from the sixth until the ninth century, known as the Great Turan.—Ed.

57 Costanzo Preve, *Filosofia e Geopolitica* (Parma: Edizioni all'insegna del Veltro, 2005). (in

Carl Schmitt's[58] terms). The policy of building socialism in one country and the growth of Soviet patriotism were essentially the next stage of continental, sovereign empire-building. And it is no accident that in the 1930s, when Stalin secured his authority, we see the distinct expression of monarchical tendencies, which constituted the peculiarity of the Russian East and the Muscovite ideology and the main impetus for the construction of a Russian Empire. Functionally, Stalin was a "Russian Czar," comparable to Peter the Great or Ivan the Terrible. In its new historical phase, the USSR continued and developed the geopolitical processes of a land-based civilization on a previously unparalleled scale, and created the state of Great Turan. The Eurasian great-continental substance is hidden under socialist forms.

The transfer of the capital of Soviet Russia from Saint Petersburg to Moscow by the Bolsheviks on March 12, 1918, was symbolic. And although this measure was dictated by practical considerations, on the level of historical parallels it signified a substantial shift toward the Russian East and thus toward the Moscow canons of land-based geopolitics. The USSR was a new version of the Russian land-based Czardom, and Stalin was the "Red Czar." The conception of the Third Rome during the Middle Ages was paradoxically transformed into the idea of Moscow as the capital of the Third International.[59] As a network of Communist parties and movements oriented toward Soviet Russia, the Third International became *a geopolitical instrument* for the propagation of land-based, tellurocratic

---

58 Carl Schmitt (1888–1985) was an important German jurist who wrote about political science, geopolitics and constitutional law. He was part of the Conservative Revolutionary movement of the Weimar era. He also briefly supported the National Socialists at the beginning of their regime, although they later turned against him. He remains highly influential in the fields of law and philosophy. He introduces the terms Leviathan and Behemoth in his book, *Land and Sea* (Washington: Plutarch Press, 1997).—Ed.

59 The Third Communist International, or Comintern as it was known, was established in Moscow 1919 with the intention of fomenting Communist revolutions throughout the world, its ultimate aim being the establishment of global Communism. It replaced the Second International, which had collapsed under the pressures of the First World War. It was dissolved in 1943 on the grounds that the problems of revolution in each nation around the world were too complex to be handled centrally.—Ed.

Russian influence worldwide. In terms of ideology, this was a territorially unbound, international, planetary network. But it terms of strategy, the Third International fulfilled the function of a geopolitical instrument for the expansion of the Heartland's geopolitical zone of influence. The Orthodox messianism of the sixteenth century was reflected wonderfully in the Bolshevist Communist "messianism" of global revolution with its core in Moscow, the capital of the Third International.

The Geopolitics of the Great Patriotic War

After the Nazis came to power in 1933, a new geopolitical balance of power took effect in the world. On one hand, there was the powerful Eurasian great-continental Soviet Union, ruled autocratically by Joseph Stalin. This is the Heartland, the core of the global continental force.

In the West, two blocs of governments form anew, as at the end of the First World War:

1. The thalassocratic alliance of England, France and the USA, and the countries of Eastern Europe that belonged to the *cordon sanitaire* and were under the control of thalassocracy (Poland, Czechoslovakia);
2. The European continental, tellurocratic states, led by Nazi Germany and Fascist Italy and by the countries occupied by them or their allies.

In the East we had Japan, aligned with Germany, underscoring Japan's tellurocratic orientation. China was in an exceedingly weakened condition and was to a significant degree controlled by the English.

In such a situation, we can, theoretically, imagine the following alliances that might have come about in the inexorably approaching war:

1. *A realization of "the continental bloc" along Haushofer's model.* This proposes an alliance of the USSR with Nazi Germany and with the other countries of the Axis and Japan. There are specific antecedents for this in the Germanophilic orientation of the Bolsheviks (the Communist

Karl Radek[60] and the German National Bolsheviks[61] — in particular, Ernst Niekisch[62] — insisted on a union of the Leftist nationalists and the USSR in an anti-bourgeois, anti-Western, anti-French and anti-English strategic harmonization),[63] in geopolitical analysis and in the fact that both regimes are nominally "socialist" and "anti-capitalist." But dogmatic Marxism, Stalin's internationalism, and Hitler's racist (anti-Communist and Judeo-phobic) worldview prevented this. The Molotov-Ribbentrop Pact[64] was a step toward such an alliance. If we admit that it could have taken place, then, most likely, the balance of powers would have been enough to crush the planetary might of thalassocracy and to take Britain and the USA out of history for a long time. Objective geopolitics urged the major continental players toward precisely such an alliance. This objective geopolitics had its conscious and systematic representatives in Germany (the school of K. Haushofer), but not in Russia. We must notice that in Germany, too,

---

60 Karl Radek (1885–1939) was a Polish Jew who was active in Marxist and Communist circles in Poland, Germany and Russia over the course of his life. In December 1918 he went to Germany, at the behest of the Bolsheviks, and aided efforts to foment a Communist revolution there. Radek was sympathetic to the activities of the Nazis and other Right-wing groups during his time there. He later returned to Russia and became an enemy of Stalin, and died as a prisoner in a labor camp.—Ed.

61 National Bolshevik ideology emerged in Germany after the First World War as an attempt to synthesise Communism and nationalism. It was formulated by some of the participants in Germany's Conservative Revolution, such as Ernst Jünger and Ernst Niekisch.—Ed.

62 Ernst Niekisch (1889–1967) was a German politician who was initially a Communist, but by the 1920s sought to merge Communism with nationalism. He published a journal, *Widerstand* (Resistance), and applied the term National Bolshevik to himself and his followers. He rejected National Socialism as insufficiently socialist, and was imprisoned by them in 1937, and became blind. Upon his release in 1945, he supported the Soviet Union and moved to East Germany, but became disillusioned by the Soviets' treatment of workers and returned to the West in 1953.—Ed.

63 Mikhail Agursky, *The Ideology of National-Bolshevism* (Moscow: Algorithm, 2003).

64 The Molotov-Ribbentrop Pact, named after the respective foreign ministers of the Soviet Union and the Third Reich, was an agreement between the two powers in which the Soviets pledged not to get involved in any European conflict, while the Germans agreed to forego an alliance with Japan, which was then at war with the Soviets. Its provisions also divided Eastern Europe into zones of future German and Soviet control, paving the way for the joint German-Soviet invasion of Poland that began the Second World War. It was signed on 23 August 1939.—Ed.

the leaders of National Socialism listened to Haushofer's opinion only partially.

2. *An alliance of the Axis countries with the bourgeois-democratic regimes of the West against the USSR.* In this case we would have something analogous to the alignment of forces in the Crimean War,[65] when all Europe was consolidated against Russia. The Munich Agreement[66] was a step in this direction. England in part supported Hitler, believing it could weaken the USSR with his help. Here, would have had a thalassocratic alliance united by common hostility among the thalassocratic countries and Germany toward Communism and Russia-Eurasia. We could predict that the USSR would be in a desperate position, lacking foreign allies. The preconditions for a military campaign would have been not only unfavorable to the USSR, but most likely fatal. Haushofer thought of this possibility, too, and it cannot be ruled out that the strange flight of Rudolf Hess,[67] Haushofer's teacher, to England after the start of Anglo-German military clashes was a desperate attempt to arrange an alliance of Germany with England in the run-up to the inevitable conflict with the USSR.

3. *An alliance of the thalassocratic bourgeois-democratic countries with the continental Eurasian USSR against the European continentalism of Germany.* This would have been a repeat of the alignment of forces on the eve of the First World War and a second version of the Entente.

---

65 The Crimean War was fought between the Russian Empire and the empires of Britain, France, and Turkey, as well as Italy, between 1853 and 1856 to halt Russia's expansion into the territories of the Ottoman Empire. Russia was defeated.—Ed.

66 The Munich Agreement was concluded in September 1938 between Germany, Britain, France and Italy, allowing Germany to seize control of large portions of Czechoslovakia.—Ed.

67 Rudolf Hess (1894–1987) had held the position of Deputy *Führer* since 1933, effectively being the most powerful man in the National Socialist hierarchy after Hitler himself. Concerned that Germany would be faced with a war on two fronts following the imminent invasion of the USSR, Hess flew to Scotland on 10 May 1941 in the hope of conducting peace negotiations with the British. Upon arrival, he was arrested and remained imprisoned for the rest of his life. Hitler denied any foreknowledge of Hess' flight and condemned it, although some historians have alleged that it may have been sanctioned by both Hitler and the British government as part of a secret negotiation that failed.—Ed.

Today we know that this scenario was in fact enacted. This happened primarily because of Hitler's suicidal adventure, a war on two fronts against both the West and the East. Ultimately, the winners could only be the countries of the West, since a conflict of two continental states with each another (like with Napoleon's invasion) entailed their mutual weakening.

Thus, the representatives of three geopolitical powers and three ideologies clashed against each other in the Second World War. The Heartland was represented by Soviet Russia, Stalin, and socialism (Marxism). The sea power, in the coalition of England, the USA and France, was united under a liberal bourgeois-democratic ideology. The continental power of Europe (Central Europe) was represented by the Axis countries (the Third Reich, Fascist Italy and their satellites) and by the ideology of the "Third Way" (National Socialism, Fascism, and Japanese samurai traditionalism). Irreconcilable and having no common ideological points of intersection at all, the poles — the USSR and the Western capitalist countries, representing respectively the Land and Sea — proved a barricade against Central Europe and National Socialism. This alignment of forces entirely *contradicts* the context and regularities of objective geopolitics. So it shows the powerful influence of the subjective factor: Hitler's personal adventurism and the effective work of anti-German agents in the USSR and anti-Soviet agents in Germany.

The timeline of the Great Patriotic War, which began on June 22, 1941, and ended on May 9, 1945, is known to every Russian.

The first stage of the war (repeating the story of Napoleon's invasion) was a relatively successful blitzkrieg by German troops, leading the German divisions to Moscow by November 1941. By December 1, German troops seized Lithuania, Latvia, Belarus, Moldova, Estonia, a significant part of the Russian Soviet Federative Socialist Republic (RSFSR),[68] and Ukraine,

---

68 This Republic was the largest and most central of the various Soviet republics comprising the USSR, and included the territory of Russia itself.—Ed.

and advanced as deep as 850–1200 kilometers. As the result of fierce resistance, the German armies were stopped in all directions at the end of November and beginning of December. The attempt to take Moscow failed. During the winter campaign of 1941–1942, a counter-offensive was carried out in Moscow. The threat to Moscow was removed. Soviet troops threw the enemy 80–250 kilometers back to the west, completed the liberation of the Moscow and Tula districts, and liberated many regions of the Klinsky and Melensky districts. On the southern front, Soviet troops defended the strategically important Crimea.

A change began in the autumn of 1942. On November 19, 1942, the counter-offensive of Soviet troops began. And from the start of 1943, Soviet troops were moving resolutely westward. The decisive events of the summer-autumn campaign of 1943 were the Battle of Kursk and the Battle of the Dnieper. The Red Army advanced 500–1300 kilometers.

From November 28 until December 1, 1943, the Tehran Conference of Stalin, Churchill, and Roosevelt[69] took place, where the major question was the opening of a second front. The Allies agreed about the fundamental direction of the future world order after the likely defeat of Germany and the Axis countries.

It is telling that Mackinder published his last geopolitical policy paper, "The Round World and the Winning of the Peace," in the American journal *Foreign Affairs*.[70] In it, he sketched the general traits and the structure of the geopolitical balance of power toward which the thalassocratic countries (the USA, England, France, and others) must strive after the victory over Germany together with such geopolitically and ideologically troublesome allies as the USSR and Stalin. Again, Mackinder, now in new circumstances, called for a blockade against the USSR, the containment of its westward movement, and the recreation of a *cordon sanitaire* in Eastern Europe.

---

69 The Tehran Conference was the first of several conferences when the leaders of the major Allied powers met.—Ed.

70 Halford Mackinder, "The Round World and the Winning of the Peace," *Foreign Affairs* (1943), no. 21.

The Red Army began the winter campaign of 1943–1944 with a major attack on the right flank of Ukraine (the Dnieper-Carpathian Offensive, December 24, 1943–April 17, 1944). April and May marked the Crimean Offensive (April 8–May 12). In June 1944, the Western Allies opened a second front, which worsened Germany's military position slightly, but did not exert decisive influence on the balance of powers or the course of the war. In the summer-autumn campaign of 1944, the Red Army carried out a series of large-scale operations, including the Belarusian, L'vosk-Sandomirsky, Yasso Kishinevsky, and pre-Baltic campaigns. It completed the liberation of Belarus, Ukraine, the Baltic states (except for a few regions of Latvia), and part of Czechoslovakia; it also liberated northern Zapolarye and the northern areas of Norway. Romania and Bulgaria were forced to capitulate and to declare war on Germany. In the summer of 1944, Soviet troops marched into Poland. Farther advances by elements of the Red Army began only in January 1945 with the Eastern Prussian operation, the Vistula-Oder operation, the Vienna operation, the Königsberg operation, and other operations. During the advance toward the west, Soviet troops established their control over the enormous space of Eastern Europe.

On April 25, 1945, Soviet troops first met the American troops, who had advanced from the West, along the Elbe River. On May 2, 1945, the Berlin garrison capitulated. After the capture of Berlin, Soviet troops carried out the Prague operation, the last strategic operation of the war.

At 10:43 PM Central European time on May 8, 1945, the war in Europe ended with the unconditional capitulation of Germany's armed forces. On June 24, a victory parade took place in Moscow. At the Potsdam Conference held from June until August 1945, an agreement was reached between the leaders of the USSR, Great Britain, and the USA about the post-war arrangement of Europe. In this agreement, the countries of the bourgeois West recognized the USSR's right to maintain control over Eastern Europe and the possibility of bringing pro-Soviet governments to power there. Moreover, Prussia passed into the control of the USSR, with its capital,

Berlin (the German Democratic Republic was established there). The territory of Berlin was divided into two sectors; the eastern part was under the control of the USSR, and the western part was under the control of the troops of the Western Allies and was united to West Germany (the Federal Republic of Germany).

The following European countries were in the zone of high-priority Soviet influence: Poland, Hungary, Romania, Yugoslavia, Czechoslovakia, Bulgaria, the German Democratic Republic, and Albania, at least at first (it later selected Maoist China as its reference point). Later, in 1955, these countries (except for Yugoslavia, which took the independent socialist "third way") also signed the Warsaw Pact, which proposed the creation of a military bloc, symmetrical to the Western bloc of capitalist countries, the North Atlantic Treaty Organization (NATO). This pact, as a visible military-strategic expression of the bipolar world, lasted until June 1, 1991.

The Geopolitical Outcomes of the Great Patriotic War

There were many geopolitical outcomes of the Great Patriotic War. The continental European power, Germany, suffered a crushing defeat, dropping off the stage of world politics for many decades. The land-based, continental element of European politics was paralyzed for a long time. Moreover, National Socialism and Fascism were decisively outlawed as ideologies, and the Nuremberg trials passed a sentence not only on Germany's political actors, held responsible for crimes against humanity, but on this ideology, branded as criminal.

Thus, in the world according to the conclusions of the Potsdam Conference, only two geopolitical and ideological forces remained: the liberal bourgeois-democratic capitalism of the West (with its core in the USA), as the pole of global thalassocracy, and the socialist, Communist, anti-bourgeois Soviet East (with its core in the USSR). We moved from a tripolar geopolitical and ideological map to a bipolar organization of global space.

From February 4 through February 11, 1945, the Yalta Conference, involving Stalin, Churchill, and Roosevelt, was held, the principles of postwar politics were discussed, and the bipolar structure of the world was formally fixed. Churchill and Roosevelt represented the Anglo-Saxon world and the American-English axis, which became a unified, strategic center, the core of Atlantic society and thalassocracy. Only Stalin spoke on behalf of the USSR as a great global Eurasian empire. This bipolar world order was called the Yalta World.

Geopolitically, this meant the establishment of *a planetary balance between the global thalassocratic and capitalist West and the equally global tellurocratic, Communist East, extending far beyond the limits of the USSR.* Moreover, the third force, represented by the European continental center and the ideology of "the Third Way," vanished for good (or at least to the present day).

The Geopolitics of the Yalta World and the Cold War

We should now pause for a geopolitical analysis of the borders between the two worlds (West and East) that were drawn on the basis of the Yalta Conference and the post-war balance of power. The structure of borders has a tremendous impact on the general balance of powers. The Belgian geopolitician and political scientist Jean Thiriart[71] first mentioned and analyzed this fact concerning the borders of the Warsaw Pact.[72] Thiriart noted that the structure of the borders between the Western and Eastern blocs, passing through the European space, was exceedingly *advantageous* for the USA and to the same degree *disadvantageous* for the USSR. This is because the security and defense of land-based borders is an exceedingly dif-

---

71 Jean Thiriart (1922–1992) was a Belgian nationalist with strong Leftist and Third World sympathies. Opposed to both the United States and the Soviet Union, he founded a movement, Jeune Europe, which sought to liberate Europe from both by cooperating with nationalist and Communist revolutionaries in the Third World. Late in life, he came to see himself as a National Bolshevik.—Ed.

72 Jean Thiriart, *Un Empire de quatre cents millions d'hommes, l'Europe* (Nantes: Avatar Editions, 2007). English edition forthcoming from Arktos.—Ed.

ficult, expensive, and resource-consuming task, especially in the case when the border is not connected to the presence of normal, natural obstacles such as mountains, river basins, and so forth — all the more so when we are considering a sociologically homogeneous society (ethnically, culturally, religiously, and so forth) on both sides of the border. The border between the countries of the Warsaw Pact, a continuation of the USSR and a continental tellurocracy, and the countries of NATO, the strategic satellites of the USA, was such a border. By contrast, the USA was safely secured by the oceans that surround its borders, which do not demand large resources or expenses to defend and permit focus on other strategic problems. In the case of a conflict with the USSR, the USA would have lost the territory of Western Europe if necessary, but its own territory was left out of reach. The USSR, however, was forced to defend the borders of the Warsaw Pact as its own.

This created unequal starting conditions for the victors of the Second World War, giving powerful strategic superiority to the USA and the NATO bloc. Understanding this, Stalin, and especially Beria,[73] who spoke of this more openly, elaborated plans in the early 1950s for the "Finlandization of Europe"; the creation of a bloc of governments in Eastern and Central Europe that would be neutral toward the USSR and NATO. This would allow a different structuring of borders. The wider this "neutral" European zone would be, the more comfortable European borders would be for Russia. At the end of the 1960s, Jean Thiriart predicted the inevitable collapse of the USSR, should the structure of borders in Europe remain unchanged. But he also proposed another scenario: the creation of a "Euro-Soviet empire from Vladivostok to Dublin";[74] a broadening of the borders

---

73 Lavrentiy Beria (1899–1953) was a Soviet politician who was in charge of the NKVD (secret police) from 1938, during the Great Purge, until 1946, and was then Deputy Premier. He was tried and executed for treason shortly after Stalin's death.—Ed.

74 Jean Thiriart, *Euro-Soviet Empire*. This book was never completed and never published. Claudio Mutti's biography of Thiriart, which includes a discussion of the uncompleted project, is online at http://www.eurasia-rivista.org/the-struggle-of-jean-thiriart/13850/.

of the Warsaw bloc to the shores of the Atlantic. Anyway, the task consisted in *changing the structure of borders.* Although it took time after the partition of Europe between the USA and USSR, it was precisely this geopolitical factor that made itself felt in a manner catastrophic for the Eastern bloc.

Returning to the post-war period and the formation of the Yalta World, we should offer a geopolitical analysis of the "Cold War." Two years after the victory over Hitler, relations between the victors of the Second World War began to worsen rapidly. Here, objective geopolitics made itself felt: the alliance of the Western thalassocratic democracies and the socialist Soviet tellurocracy was so unnatural, both geopolitically and ideologically, that a conflict was lying in wait in these relations from the start.

The "Cold War" began in 1947, when the American diplomat George F. Kennan[75] published a text in *Foreign Affairs* calling for the *containment* of the USSR. Kennan, a follower of Mackinder, the American geopolitician Nicholas Spykman, and Robert Strausz-Hupé,[76] elaborated a model of a configuration of global zones, controlled by the USA, that would inevitably and steadily lead America to the domination of Eurasia. The strangulation of the USSR in the inner-continental space of Eurasia and the restriction and blockade of Soviet influence worldwide were part of this strategy. The main strategy consisted in *enclosing* the coastal zone (Rimland) within itself, under the control of the USA in the space of Eurasia, from Western Europe through the Middle East and Central Asia to the Far East, India, and Indo-China. Japan, occupied by the USA, was already a fulcrum for American naval strategy.

The USSR reacted to this strategy and, in turn, tried to break the control of the USA and NATO over the coastal zone (Rimland). Evidence of this reaction can be seen in the harsh confrontation that occurred dur-

---

75 George F. Kennan (1904–2005) was an American diplomat whose views were highly influential upon America's geopolitical strategy towards the Soviet Union in the early years of the Cold War.—Ed.

76 Robert Stausz-Hupé (1904–2002) was an American diplomat who was regarded as a hardliner during the Cold War.—Ed.

ing the time of Vietnam, the Korean War, and the Chinese Revolution, actively supported by the USSR. Moreover, the USSR supported socialist tendencies in the Islamic world, in particular "Arab socialism,"[77] and gave support to pro-Soviet Communist parties in Western Europe. The great war of the civilization of the Sea and the civilization of Land was also carried to other continents, Africa and Latin America. In Africa this involved Angola, Ethiopia, Somalia, and Mozambique (afro-Communism); in Latin America, it was Cuba and the powerful Communist movements in Chile, Argentina, Peru, Venezuela, and elsewhere.

The factor of nuclear weapons was of tremendous importance in the "Cold War." The USA's new weapon, successfully deployed in the attacks on Hiroshima and Nagasaki, seemed to give them a decisive advantage in a future confrontation with the USSR. Stalin focused his efforts on getting the same weapon for the USSR. Here, the allies of the USSR in the Communist networks across the world played an important role. The ideological commitment of Leftist sympathizers essentially made them a network of agents of influence and portals for gathering information in the interests of the civilization of Land. Thus, vital information about nuclear weapons was obtained from an American scientist, the nuclear physicist Theodore Hall,[78] through a network of Soviet agents. In tandem with Soviet research, a Soviet nuclear bomb was quickly and successfully constructed, levelling the technological abilities of the two superpowers.

By the 1950s, the geopolitical picture of the bipolar world, a planetary expression of Mackinder's geopolitical map, was fixed in its basic characteristics. The Heartland and the civilization of Land were represented by the USSR, the countries of the Warsaw Pact, and the socialist regimes some-

---

77 Arab socialism is a form of socialism that emerged in the Arab world in the 1940s, which combines socialism with pan-Arab nationalism. Some exemplary Arab socialist regimes have been that of Nasser in Egypt, and the Ba'athist regimes of Iraq and Syria.—Ed.

78 Theodore Hall (1925–1999), along with the British scientist Klaus Fuchs, worked on the Manhattan Project, and passed atomic secrets to the Soviets. Although he was questioned by the FBI, no definitive proof of his subversion was discovered until decades later.—Ed.

times far from the USSR. This was the Soviet superpower and its zone of influence. Land reached its *historical maximum* and a previously unthinkable scope and scale of influence. Eurasia became a world empire, spreading the networks of its influence on a global scale.

The other superpower, the USA, also became the center of a global hegemony. The NATO bloc and the capitalist countries worldwide sided with it. Between these two planetary powers, "the great war of continents" was enacted from then on, formed ideologically as the opposition between *capitalism and Communism*. Thalassocracy was identified with the bourgeois-capitalist model and with the market society (of the Athenian, Carthaginian type); tellurocracy with the socialist society of the Spartan-Roman type. All the major players were distributed along these two poles. Those who wavered in the selection of their geopolitical and ideological orientation cheered the "Non-Aligned Movement." But this Movement did not represent a fully-fledged third pole, nor did it work out any kind of independent ideological platform or geopolitical strategy. Rather, these countries were "no man's lands" or neutral territories, where representatives of the Eastern and Western blocs operated with equal success.

The bipolar world aimed at in the Potsdam Conference and fixed at the Yalta Conference became the basic model of international relations for a few decades, from the 1950s until 1991; until the end of the USSR.

The Yalta World after the Death of Stalin

Stalin was a classic figure in the tradition of the great-continental leader, exactly suited for both the scale of the geopolitical tasks standing before Russia in the twentieth century and for the sociological constants of Eurasian tellurocractic sociology, oriented toward hierarchical, vertical, "heroic," and "Spartan" values. It is difficult to say whether he was thoroughly familiar with the ideas of the Eurasianists and the National Bolsheviks and whether he had a precise notion of geopolitical patterns. Anyhow, a precise and distinct logic is visible in his foreign policy. Each action was directed toward strengthening the power of the civilization of Land, expanding the Soviet government's zone of influence, and defending strategic interests. During his rule, a consistent Eurasian geopolitical policy was consciously implemented. A few of his associates differed strongly by their clear understanding of the patterns of international processes, closely associated with the geopolitical context; in particular, Vyacheslav Molotov,[79] Beria, and others. It seems that after Stalin's death and Beria's removal from power, the Soviet leadership's geopolitical self-consciousness weakened abruptly. They continued to act within the framework of the bipolar world and tried to secure the Soviet pole and, as much as possible, use all US oversights to strengthen pro-Soviet tendencies throughout the world. However, Soviet foreign policy then became reactive, secondary, and, in the most cases, defensive.

It is important that during Khrushchev's rule and afterwards, Soviet leaders lost their concern with the condition of European borders. If this problem concerned Stalin and Beria, it seems that afterward, Soviet leaders forgot it, prioritizing other questions.

Under Khrushchev, the Caribbean crisis broke out, caused by the Cuban Revolution. On the whole, this revolution was a symmetrical response to the geopolitical Atlanticism of the USA in Eurasia: as America tried to place their military bases close to the territory of the USSR in the coastal zone of the Eurasian mainland, so Castro's Cuba, escaping the control of the USA and carrying out a proletarian revolution, logically transformed into a strategic base of Soviet presence near the USA. Thus, when the USSR decided to deploy nuclear missiles in Cuba in October 1962, this was entirely natural, especially when one considers the placement of medium-range "Jupiter" rockets in Turkey by the USA in 1961, directly threat-

---

79 Vyacheslav Molotov (1890–1986) was a leading Bolshevik from before the time of the Russian Revolution in 1917. He most famously served as the Soviet Union's Minister of Foreign Affairs from 1939–1949 and again from 1953–1956. He spearheaded the USSR's treaty with the Third Reich in 1939. He defended the policies of the Stalinist era until his death,—Ed.

ening cities in the western Soviet Union, rockets that could reach Moscow and the major industrial centers.

When an American U2 spy plane discovered P-12 medium-range Soviet missiles in the outskirts of San Cristóbal, supposedly equipped with nuclear warheads, the "Cold War" nearly developed into a nuclear conflict between the two superpowers. At first President Kennedy decided to begin a massive bombardment of Cuba, but it became apparent that the Soviet missiles were in combat readiness and ready for an attack on the USA. After intense negotiations, the USSR was obligated to dismantle its missiles for US guarantees to renounce any interventions on the island.

Geopolitically, the Cuban Missile Crisis signified the culmination of the great war of continents: a point of such tension that a global nuclear war was the most likely outcome. The aftermath of the crisis resulted in both superpowers following the path of deténte, afraid of the nuclear destruction of humanity.[80]

In its domestic policy, Khrushchev's era was marked by the dethronement of Stalin's cult of personality and by the criticism of his style of leadership. This phenomenon received the name "the thaw." In this period, the dissident movement began to form in the USSR, and its representatives adopted a pro-Western position and started to criticize socialism and the "totalitarian" Soviet society. It is important to emphasize that geopolitically, most dissidents considered Western society and capitalism *a model for imitation* and Soviet society *an object of criticism*, which allows us to characterize them as carriers of the Atlanticist, thalassocratic principle. Among the dissidents were also patriotic, nationally oriented personalities (the aca-

---

80 Détente refers to the period of the lessening of tensions between the Soviet Union and the United States, which began in the late 1960s and continued through the 1970s, marked by an increased willingness of both parties to compromise in order to preserve peace.—Ed.

demic Igor Shafarevich,[81] U. Osipov, G. Shimonov, and so on), but overall they were the minority.

In foreign policy, Khrushchev lost an important ally in Maoist China, whose leadership responded very unfavorably to the dethronement of the cult of Stalin and his political policy in general. On the whole, Khrushchev's foreign policy repeated the main force-lines of the USSR's traditional policy.

After Khrushchev's dismissal from the office of General Secretary, Leonid Ilyich Brezhnev[82] came to power for two decades. The policies of this period were distinguished by conservatism and the absence of change. On one hand, a return to Stalinism did not occur, but the harsh criticism of his cult of personality was cut back, too. Khrushchev's thaw was also ended, and the dissident movement was subjected to serious pressure by the KGB and its use of punitive psychiatry. In foreign policy, Brezhnev sought to elude direct confrontation with the West.

But in 1965, the USA invaded Vietnam to support the capitalist and pro-Western regime of South Vietnam, which had its capital in Saigon. Opposing it was a pro-Soviet political system in North Vietnam, established even earlier (in 1945 Ho Chi Minh proclaimed the creation of the independent Democratic Republic of Vietnam, from which a war conducted by the French tore away the southern part, dividing the country in two), with its capital in Hanoi. China came out on the side of the Vietcong (North Vietnam). The USSR, too, gave Hanoi significant support. On April 30, 1975, the Communists lifted their banner over the Palace of Independence in Saigon.

---

81 Igor Shafarevich (b. 1923) is a mathematician, also known for a book he published in 1980, *The Socialist Phenomenon*, which claimed that socialism was inherently anti-individualistic and nihilistic. In 1982 he wrote a book called Russophobia, in which he claimed that elites with values different from those of the cultures they inhabit come to power and initiate reforms in nations, saying that the Jews occupied this role in the Russian Revolution.—Ed.

82 Leonid Brezhnev (1906–1982) was Premier of the Soviet Union from 1964 until his death. His tenure, especially the latter part of it, marked a period of increasing economic and social stagnation and increasing Soviet aggression in foreign affairs.—Ed.

Geopolitically, this was a typical battle between thalassocracy and tel-lurocracy for control over the coastal zone (Rimland). The Americans tried to establish their influence there; pro-Soviet forces strove to free them-selves from this influence in favor of the continental USSR. The failure of American intervention was a major tactical victory for the USSR. The Soviet bloc emerged from this episode of the great war of continents as the conqueror.

The situation in Afghanistan, where Soviet troops had to intervene in 1979, turned out differently. By this time, the domestic political at-mosphere in the USSR had qualitatively worsened: apathy and indiffer-ence dominated Soviet society. The ideological clichés of socialism and Marxism, repeated endlessly, started to lose their meaning; stagnation and indifference ascended the throne. The totalitarian elements of the Soviet system became grotesque. The lack of intense repressions, which stopped after Stalin's time, did not lead to the rise of creativity or the mobilization of dynamic energies, but only weakened the populace. Narrow-minded and consumerist motives began to prevail in society. The cultural sphere de-graded abruptly. In this context, Soviet troops invaded Afghanistan to pro-vide assistance to the Soviet-oriented leadership of Taraki.[83] On April 27, 1978, the April Revolution began in Afghanistan, as a result of which the People's Democratic Party of Afghanistan came to power. In September 1979 a *coup d'etat* occurred, during which Hafizullah Amin[84] came to pow-er, oriented toward closer relations with the USA. Soviet troops entered Kabul and stormed Amin's palace, destroying him and his associates. The pro-Soviet leader Babrak Karmal[85] was brought to power. Soon, opposition

---

83 Nur Muhammad Taraki (1917–1979) was a socialist who was President of Afghanistan from April 1978, when he came to power following a coup, until he was deposed and murdered, which was one of the catalysts for the subsequent Soviet occupation.—Ed.

84 Hafizullah Amin (1929–1979), although a Communist, attempted to orient Afghanistan away from the Soviet Union. The Soviets, alarmed by this, sent in troops and accused Amin of being a CIA agent. He was killed in the subsequent fighting.—Ed.

85 Babrak Karmal (1929–1996) was President of Afghanistan from the end of 1979 until 1986.—Ed.

to Karmal's regime expanded throughout the country, led by the representatives of various Islamic groups, primarily, fundamentalists. There, too, the "Al-Qaeda" of Osama bin Laden was formed and later became famous. By the logic of objective geopolitics, once the USSR stood behind Karmal, the leaders of the Central Intelligence Agency (CIA) appeared behind his opponents, the Islamists. In particular, the major American geopolitician Zbigniew Brzezinski,[86] the direct successor to the geopolitical, thalassocratic policy of Mackinder and Spykman, provided support to the Islamic *mujahideen* in Afghanistan. In April 1980, the US Congress openly authorized "direct and open support" for the Afghan opposition.

Like the Korean and the Vietnam War, the Afghanistan War was a typical confrontation of tellurocracy and thalassocracy in a fight for influence over the coastal zone. The territory of Afghanistan does not have any warm-water ports, but it closely adjoins the borders of the USSR and was for that reason strategically important for the entire strategy of the containment of the USSR, on which the strategy of the USA was based during the entire "Cold War." At the end of the nineteenth century and start of the twentieth, Afghanistan was already becoming a stumbling block for Russian-British relations, and a very important element of the "Great Game."[87] The outstanding Russian strategist Andrei Snesarev[88] wrote about the strategic significance of Afghanistan for the Russian Empire.[89]

---

86 Zbigniew Brzezinski (b. 1928) was the National Security Advisor during the Carter administration. He was a hawk on the Soviet Union and began to move the United States away from the policy of détente with the Soviets that it had been following.—Ed.

87 The Great Game refers to the competition between the British and Russian empires for influence in Afghanistan, which continued from the early nineteenth until the early twentieth century.—Ed.

88 Andrei Sensarev (1865–1937) was a Russian general who volunteered for the Red Army during the Russian Revolution. Having earlier served throughout the Middle East and Asia, he became the head of the Institute of Oriental Studies in Moscow following his military career.—Ed.

89 Andrei Snesarev, *Afghanistan: Preparing for the Bolshevik Incursion into Afghanistan and Attack on India, 1919–20* (Helion & Company, 2014).

Brezhnev, during whose reign a definite stability and conservatism reigned in the USSR, died in 1982, at the very height of the Afghanistan War, in which Soviet troops suffered serious losses, but overall remained in control of the situation. In his place came the former head of the KGB, Yuri Andropov.[90] His short rule (he died in 1984) did not leave a considerable mark. Konstantin Chernenko[91] took his place, but died in 1985, without having had time to designate his own policy.

In general, from the death of Stalin to the death of Chernenko, the Soviet leadership worked within the bipolar model of the world that took shape as a result of the Second World War. This period marked the positional confrontation of the civilization of Land (the Eastern bloc) with the civilization of the Sea (the Western bloc) on a previously unprecedented global scale, when the zone of this game was almost the entire Earth.

Theories of Convergence and Globalism

To understand the events of the 1980s that took place in the USSR and the world, it is necessary to turn our attention to a group of theories that appeared in the West in the 1970s and that had a tremendous influence on the following course of events. Theories of convergence began to be formulated in the 1950s and 1960s among sociologists and economists (Pitirim Sorokin, James Gilbert, Raymond Aron, Jan Tinbergen, and others). They claimed that, according to the measure of technological development, the capitalist and socialist systems would in time draw closer and closer together. In capitalist societies, they held, the role of central planning in

---

90 Yuri Andropov (1914–1984) was a Communist from his teenage years and, as ambassador to Hungary, helped to crush the 1956 revolution there. He was appointed head of the KGB in 1967, and assisted the violent suppression of the Prague Spring uprising, and became a member of the Politburo in 1973. He worked for the suppression of Soviet dissidents abroad and was also the main proponent of the intervention in Afghanistan in 1979. He became General Secretary in November 1982 but only held the position for 15 months, prior to his death.—Ed.

91 Konstantin Chernenko (1911–1985) was a lifelong Communist who had been a member of the Central Committee since 1965.—Ed.

technological processes was increasing; in the socialist economy, small private ownership structures were beginning to appear (for instance, in the countries of Eastern Europe). Supporters of this theory thought that competition between the two global systems would eventually have to yield to a general, integrated system of a mixed type, part capitalist and part socialist.

After the Cuban Missile Crisis and in the period of deténte in the relations between the two blocs, these theories acquired a practical significance, as they established a common canvas for drawing together socialist countries and capitalist ones.

Parallel to this development, a few organizations arose in the West that put before themselves the task of a *global* comprehension of the problems facing humanity without taking stock of its division into East and West, capitalism and socialism. Thus in 1968, the Italian industrialist Aurelio Peccei[92] and the eminent scientist Alexander King[93] founded the Club of Rome, an organization uniting the representatives of the global political, financial, cultural, and scientific elite, which placed before itself the task of a global analysis of world problems. Soviet scientists were also drawn into the Club of Rome (in particular, the academic Dzhermen Gvishiani,[94] the director of the Institute of Systems Analysis of the Russian Academy of Sciences).[95]

A global view of humanity and the project of establishing a "world government" also drove the conceptual strategy of such influential organizations as the American Council on Foreign Relations and the international

---

92 Aurelio Peccei (1908–1984) had worked for the Italian automotive company Fiat since the 1930s, and also became President of the Italian office supply company Olivetti in 1964. During the Fascist period he was involved in opposition activities. Peccei was also instrumental in integrating the findings of the 1972 study *Limits to Growth*, which held that a growing world population and dwindling resources would eventually lead to a civilizational collapse, into the Club of Rome's outlook.—Ed.

93 Alexander King (1909–2007) was a British chemist who helped to found the sustainable development movement.—Ed.

94 Alexander Shevyakin, *The Mystery of the Death of the USSR* (Moscow: Veche, 2004).

95 Founded in 1976 as a branch of the International Institute of Applied Systems Analysis (IIASA) under the Club of Rome; the main subdivision of the IIASA was in Vienna.

"Trilateral Commission," founded on this basis. These organizations tried to establish special relations with the Soviet political leadership, proposing a consolidation of efforts for further deténte and the resolution of problems common to mankind.

It is important to pay attention to the "Trilateral Commission." This organization, founded by the CFR under the aegis of David Rockefeller and the eminent political scientists and geopoliticians Zbigniew Brzezinski and Henry Kissinger, united the representatives of three geopolitical zones — America, Europe, and Japan — considered the three centers of the capitalist system, the civilization of the Sea. The task of this organization, whose activity was surrounded by a veil of secrecy, consisted in coordinating the efforts of the leading capitalist countries for victory in the "Cold War," and isolating the USSR and its allies from all sides: from the West (Europe), from the East (Japan), and from the south (the allies of the USA and NATO among the Middle Eastern and Asian regimes). But the "Trilateral Commission" did not only use the tactic of head-on confrontation; it also tried to seduce the adversary into dialogue. So, at the end of the 1970s and the beginning of the 1980s, the representatives of this organization began offering assistance to China in the production of a new, liberal economic policy, and made a sizeable investment in its economy to support its development, despite its Communist regime. This was done with the goal of further tearing China away from the USSR and strengthening its own influence in the Far East, to the detriment of Soviet influence. It is very characteristic that this globalist club was founded primarily on the model of the CFR, the structure that had pioneered the rapid development of geopolitics in the USA already at the time of Versailles, and with which the founder of geopolitics, Halford Mackinder, had worked closely in the last years of his life. The idea of uniting the three principle cores of the capitalist world into a single, coordinated center had already been expressed during the creation of the CFR at Versailles. At that time the discussion was about the organization of a corresponding structure in Europe, particularly in

England, where the Royal Institute of Strategic Studies (Chatham House)[96] was to fulfill this function (and this was realized), and of the creation of an "Institute of Pacific Studies" (this was not). Projects about the global governance of the world in the interests of the civilization of the Sea, therefore, started to form in the 1920s, in parallel with the new geopolitical course of Woodrow Wilson. The first organizational subdivisions were formed to assist in the realization of these projects. We see a new branch of similar initiatives in the 1970s in the creation of the "Trilateral Commission."

Geopolitically, and with an eye to the fact that it was a question of the deep opposition of the civilization of Land against the civilization of the Sea, the aspiration to draw the capitalist and socialist systems together (to reconcile Land and Sea) on an economic, ideological, and practical level was an exceedingly contradictory strategy, which had three theoretically possible explanations:

1. Either it was the cunning of the civilization of the Sea to put the watchfulness of the civilization of Land to sleep and to compel the USSR to make ideological and other concessions to the West;

2. or it was a large-scale special operation of Soviet Communist groups of influence in Western countries, striving to weaken the civilization of the Sea and to unobtrusively compel it to recognize the same set of values as the civilization of Land (socialism, centralized planning);

3. or it was a sincere wish to bring to a close "the great war of continents" and to unite Land and Sea in an unprecedented and unimaginable synthesis.

In the first case, the strategy of convergence was intended to weaken the USSR and, possibly, bring about its fall. In the second, it was to have has-

---

96 Chatham House is a non-profit, non-governmental organization founded in 1920 for the scientific study of international affairs that emerged from discussions at the Versailles peace conference. It established the Chatham House Rule, which states that participants in one of their events can freely discuss their seminars, but that they cannot identify the speakers or reproduce the statements exactly, in order to allow speakers to feel free to be more frank.—Ed.

tened the prospects of world revolution and the fall of the capitalist system (the ascent to power of Leftist forces). In the third, it was meant to bring about the appearance of a new utopian ideology, based on a complete overcoming of geopolitics and its dual symmetry.

Today we know perfectly well how the interest in this theory and these institutions ended for the USSR, but in the 1960s and 1970s, both the supporters and the opponents of convergence could only guess at its actual content and at the results that would come when it would be carried out.

Beginning in the 1970s, theories of globalization began to take shape, based on predictions about the unification of humanity into a single social system (One World) with a common statehood (World State) and world leadership (World Government). But the concrete structure and principles on which this "one world" would have to be based remained approximate, as the outcome of the "Cold War" was still undecided. This could have been world capitalism (the victory of the civilization of the Sea), world socialism (the victory of the civilization of Land and the success of the world revolution), or some kind of mixed variant (the theory of convergence and the marginal, humanistic projects being carried out in the spirit of the Club of Rome, based on foresight about "the limits of growth," ecology, pacifism, predictions of the exhaustibility of natural resources, and so on).

The Geopolitics of Perestroika

Until 1985, the attitude in the USSR toward the idea of drawing closer to the West was generally skeptical. This only changed slightly under Andropov. On his instructions, a group of Soviet scientists and academic institutes were given the task of cooperating with globalist structures (the Club of Rome, the CFR, the Trilateral Commission, and others). Overall, however, the principal foreign policy aims of the USSR remained unchanged during the entire stretch from Stalin to Chernenko.

Changes in the USSR began with Gorbachev's assumption of the office of General Secretary of the Communist Party of the Soviet Union. He took office against the backdrop of the Afghanistan War, which was more and more developing into a deadlock. From his first steps in the office of General Secretary, Gorbachev encountered major problems. The social, economic, political, and ideological car began to stall. Soviet society was in a state of apathy. The Marxist worldview had lost its appeal and only continued to be broadcast by inertia. A growing percentage of the urban intelligentsia became increasingly attracted to Western culture and wished for "Western" standards. The outskirts of the nation lost its potential for modernization, and in some places the reverse processes of anti-modernization began; nationalist sentiments flared up, and so on. The arms race and the necessity of constantly competing with a rather dynamically developing capitalist system exhausted the economy. To an even greater extent, discontent in the socialist countries of Eastern Europe, where the appeal of the Western capitalist lifestyle was felt even more keenly, reached an apex, while the prestige of the USSR gradually fell. In these conditions, Gorbachev had to make a decision about the future strategy of the USSR and of the entire Eastern bloc.

And he did make it. The decision was to adopt as a foundation, in a difficult situation, *the theories of convergence and the propositions of the globalist groups and to begin drawing closer to the Western world through one-sided concessions.* Most likely, Gorbachev and his advisors expected symmetrical actions from the West: the West should have responded to each of Gorbachev's concessions with analogous movements in favor of the USSR. This algorithm was inherent in the foundations of the policy of perestroika. In domestic policy, this meant the abandonment of the strict ideological Marxist dictatorship, the relaxation of restrictions of non-Marxist philosophical and scientific theories, the cessation of pressure on religious institutions (primarily the Russian Orthodox Church), a broadening of permissible interpretations of Soviet history, a policy of the creation of small private enterprises (cooperatives), and the freer association of citizens with shared political and ideological interests. In this sense, perestroika was a chain of steps directed toward the adoption of democracy, parliamentism, the market, "*glasnost*," and the expansion of zones of civic freedom. This was a movement *away from the socialist model of society and toward a bour-geois-democratic and capitalist model*. But at first this movement was grad-ual and remained in a social-democratic framework; democratization and liberalism were combined with the preservation of the party model of the administration of the country, a strict vertical and planned economy, and the control of the party agencies and special services that administered so-ciopolitical processes.

However, in other countries of the Eastern bloc, and on the periphery of the USSR itself, these transformations were perceived as a manifesta-tion of weakness and as unilateral concessions to the West. This conclusion was confirmed by Gorbachev's decision to finally remove all Soviet mili-tary forces from Afghanistan in 1989, by his vacillations over the series of democratic revolutions that unfolded throughout Eastern Europe, and by his inconsistent policies toward to the allied republics: Estonia, Lithuania and Latvia, and Georgia and Armenia, the first republics involved in the establishment of independent statehood.

Against this background, the West took up a well-defined position: while they encouraged Gorbachev and his reforms in word only and ex-tolled his fateful undertaking, no symmetrical step was taken in favor of the USSR; not the smallest concession was made in any area to Soviet politi-cal, strategic, and economic interests. So, by 1991 Gorbachev's policies led to the gigantic, planetary system of Soviet influence being *brought down*, while the vacuum of control was quickly filled by the second pole, the USA and NATO. And if in the first stages of perestroika it was still possible to consider it as a special maneuver in the "Cold War" (like the plan for the "Finlandization of Europe," worked out by Beria; Gorbachev himself spoke of a "Common European House")[97] then by the end of the 1980s it became clear that we were dealing with a case of direct and one-sided *capitulation*.

Gorbachev agreed to remove all Soviet troops from the German Democratic Republic, disbanded the Warsaw Pact, recognized the legitimacy of the new bourgeois governments in the countries of Eastern Europe, and moved to meet the aspirations of the Soviet republics to receive a large degree of sovereignty and independence and to revise the agreement underlying the formation of the USSR on new terms. More and more, Gorbachev also rejected the social-democratic line, opening a path for direct bourgeois-capitalist reforms in the economy. In a word, Gorbachev's reforms amounted to *recognition of the defeat of the USSR in its confrontation with the West and the USA.*

Geopolitically, perestroika is not only a repudiation of the ideological confrontation with the capitalist world, but also a complete contradiction of Russia's entire historical path as a Eurasian, great-continental formation, as the Heartland, and as the civilization of Land. This was the undermining of Eurasia from within; the voluntary self-destruction of one of the poles of the world system; a pole that had not arisen only in the Soviet period, but which had taken shape over centuries and millennia according to the natural logic of geopolitical history and the rules of objective geopolitics. Gorbachev took the position of Westernism, which quickly led to the collapse of the global structure and to a new version of the Time of Troubles.[98] Instead of Eurasianism, Atlanticism was adopted; in place of the civilization of Land and its sociological set of values was placed the normatives of the civilization of the Sea, which were contrary to it in all respects. If we compare the geopolitical significance of these reforms with other periods

---

97 In a speech he gave in Prague in April 1987, Gorbachev in which he called for a pan-European mentality that would transcend the political divisions which then divided the Continent.—Ed.

98 The Time of Troubles refers to a period between 1598 and 1613 which saw one of the worst famines in Russian history, as well as political instability, disputes over the throne, and invasion and occupation of Russian lands by the Polish–Lithuanian Commonwealth.—Ed.

in Russian history, we cannot escape the feeling that they are something unprecedented.

The Time of Troubles in Russian history did not last long, and was followed by periods of new, sovereign rebirth. Even the most frightening dissensions preserved this or that integrating political center, which became in time a pole for a new centralization of the Russian lands. And even the Russian Westernizers, oriented toward Europe, adopted ideas and mores, technologies, and skills along with European customs, used to reinforce the might of the Russian state, to secure its borders, and to assert its national interests. Thus, the Westernizer Peter or the pro-German Catherine II,[99] with all their enthusiasm for Europe, increased the territory of Russia and achieved new military victories for it. Even the Bolsheviks, obsessed by the idea of world revolution and having agreed willingly to the fettering terms of the Brest-Litovsk world, began in a short period to strengthen the Soviet Union, returning its outskirts in the west and the south under the rule of Moscow. The case of Gorbachev is an absolute exception in Russian geopolitical history. This history did not know such betrayal even in its worst periods. Not only was the socialist system destroyed; the Heartland was destroyed from within.

The Geopolitical Significance of the Collapse of the USSR

Because of the collapse of the USSR, *the Yalta World came to its logical end.* This means that the bipolar model ended. *One pole ended its own existence.* Now, one could say with certainty that the theory of convergence was *the cunning of the civilization of the Sea.* This cunning conceived an action and brought victory to thalassocracy in the "Cold War." No convergence occurred in practice, and according to the extent of the one-sided concessions from the side of the USSR, the West only strengthened its capitalist and

---

99 Catherine II (1729–1796) was Empress of the Russian Empire and presided over what came to be known as the Golden Age of Russian history. She was victorious in many wars and expanded the territory of the Empire greatly. A student of the French philosophers, she advocated for many of the ideals of the Enlightenment.—Ed.

liberal ideology, expanding its influence farther and farther throughout the ideological vacuum that had formed. Coupled with this, NATO's zone of control also expanded. Thus, at first almost all the countries of Eastern Europe joined NATO (Romania, Hungary, the Czech Republic, Slovakia, Bulgaria, Poland, Slovenia, Croatia), and later the former republics of the USSR (Estonia, Lithuania, Latvia). This means that the structure of the world after the "Cold War" *preserved one of its poles,* the civilization of the Sea, the West, Leviathan, Carthage: the bourgeois-democratic bloc with its center in the USA.

The end of the bipolar world meant, therefore, the victory of one of its poles and its strengthening at the expense of the loser. One of the poles vanished, while the other remained and became the natural dominating structure of the entire global geopolitical system. This victory of the civilization of the Sea over the civilization of the Land constitutes the essence of globalization. From now on, the world was global and unipolar. Sociologically, globalization is the planetary spreading of a single model *of Western bourgeois-democratic, liberal, market society,* the society of merchants; *thalassocracy.* The USA is the center and core of the reality of this (now global) bourgeois-democratic thalassocracy. Democratization, Westernization, Americanization, and globalism essentially represent various aspects of *the total attack by the civilization of the Sea,* the hegemony of the Sea. This was the result of the planetary duel that was the primary factor in international politics throughout the twentieth century. During Khrushchev's rule, the Soviet version of tellurocracy suffered a colossal catastrophe, and its territorial zones separating the Heartland from the warm seas came under the control of the sea power to a significant degree. That is how we should understand both the expansion of NATO in the East at the expense of the former socialist countries and allied republics and the later increase of Western influence in the post-Soviet space.

The collapse of the USSR put an end to the Soviet era of Russia's geopolitics. This drama ended with such a severe defeat that there is no analogue to it in Russia's preceding history; not even when it fell into complete dependence on the Mongols, and even that was compensated for by integration into a tellurocratic political model. In the present case, we see the awesome victory of the principal enemies of all tellurocracy, with the crippling defeat of Rome and the triumph of the new Carthage.

CHAPTER III

The Geopolitics of Yeltsin's Russia and its Sociological Significance

The Great Loss of Rome: The Vision of G. K. Chesterton

Geopolitically, the disintegration of the USSR signified an event of colossal importance, affecting the entire structure of the global geopolitical map. According to its geopolitical features, the confrontation of the West and East, the capitalist camp and the socialist one, was the peak of the deep process of the great war of continents, a planetary duel between the civilization of Land and the civilization of the Sea, raised to the highest degree of intensity. All preceding history led to the tense apogee of this battle, which reached its qualitative resolution in 1991. *Now, with the death of the USSR, the collapse of the civilization of Land was realized, the bulwark of tellurocracy fell, and the Heartland received a fatal blow.*

To understand the meaning of this pivotal moment of world history, we should recall what the English writer G. K. Chesterton said in his work *The Everlasting Man*[100] about the meaning of the victory of Rome in the

---

100 G. K. Chesterton, *The Collected Works of G. K. Chesterton*, vol. 2 (San Francisco: Ignatius Press, 1986).

series of Punic Wars[101] against Carthage. With slight abridgement, we will narrate this episode, which reflects the essence of the geopolitical understanding of world history.

> The Punic Wars once looked as if they would never end; it is not easy to say when they ever began. The Greeks and the Sicilians had already been fighting vaguely on the European side against the African city. Carthage had defeated Greece and conquered Sicily. Carthage had also planted herself firmly in Spain; between Spain and Sicily the Latin city was contained and would have been crushed; if the Romans had been of the sort to be easily crushed. Yet the interest of the story really consists in the fact that Rome was crushed. If there had not been certain moral elements alongside material elements, the story would have ended where Carthage certainly thought it had ended. It is common enough to blame Rome for not making peace. But it was a true popular instinct that there could be no peace with that sort of people. It is common enough to blame the Roman for his *Delenda est Carthago*; Carthage must be destroyed. It is commoner to forget that, to all appearance, Rome itself was destroyed. [...] Carthage was an aristocracy, as are most of such mercantile states. The pressure of the rich on the poor was impersonal and irresistible. For such aristocracies never permit personal government, which is perhaps why this one was envious of personal talent. But genius can arise anywhere, even in a governing class. As if to make the world's supreme test as terrible as possible, it was ordained that one of the great houses of Carthage should produce a man who came out of those gilded palaces with all the energy and originality of Napoleon coming from nowhere. At the worst crisis of the war Rome learned that Italy itself, by a military miracle, was invaded from the North. Hannibal, the Grace of Baal as his name ran in his own tongue, had dragged a ponderous chain of armaments over the starry solitudes of the Alps and pointed south to the city that he had been pledged by all his dreadful gods to destroy. [...]
>
> The Roman augurs and scribes who said in that hour that it brought forth unearthly prodigies, that a child was born with the head of an elephant or that stars fell like hailstones, had a far more philosophical grasp of what had happened than the modern historian who can see nothing in it but a success of strategy concluding a rivalry in commerce. Something far different was felt there and then, as it is always felt by those who experience a foreign atmosphere entering

---

101 The Punic Wars were three conflicts fought between Rome and Carthage between 264 to 146 BC. As the two powers were the greatest in the region at the time, the wars were fought on a scale seldom seen in the ancient world.—Ed.

theirs like fog or a foul stench. It was no mere military defeat, and certainly no mere mercantile rivalry, that filled the Roman imagination with such hideous omens of nature herself becoming unnatural. It was Moloch upon the mountain of the Latins, looking with his appalling face across the plain; it was Baal who trampled the vineyards with his feet of stone; it was the voice of Tanit the invisible, behind her trailing veils, whispering of the love that is more horrible than hate. The burning of the Italian cornfields and the ruin of the Italian vines were something more than real; they were allegorical. They were the destruction of domestic and fruitful things, the withering of what was human before that inhumanity that is far beyond the human thing called cruelty [...] The war of the gods and demons seemed already to have ended; the gods were dead. The eagles were lost; the legions were broken; nothing remained in Rome but honor and the cold courage of despair.One thing still threatened Carthage: Carthage itself. There remained the inner working of an element strong in all successful commercial states, and the presence of a spirit that we know. There was still the solid sense and shrewdness of the men who manage big enterprises; there was still the advice of the best financial experts; there was still business government; there was still the broad and sane outlook of practical men of affairs, and in these things could the Romans hope. As the war trailed on to what seemed its tragic end, there grew gradually a faint and strange possibility that even now they might not hope in vain. The plain businessmen of Carthage, thinking as such men do of living and dying races, saw clearly that Rome was not only dying but dead. The war was over; it was obviously hopeless for the Italian city to resist any longer and inconceivable that anybody should resist when it was hopeless. Under these circumstances, another set of broad, sound business principles had to be considered. Wars were waged with money, and so cost money; perhaps they felt in their hearts, as do so many of their kind, that after all war must be a little wicked because it costs money. The time had now come for peace, and still more for economy. The messages sent by Hannibal periodically asking for reinforcements were a ridiculous anachronism; there were much more important things to attend to now. It might be true that some consul or other had made a last dash to the Metaurus, had killed Hannibal's brother and flung his head, with Latin fury, into Hannibal's camp. Mad actions of that sort showed how utterly hopeless the Latins felt about their cause. But even excitable Latins could not be so mad to cling to a lost cause forever. So argued the best financial experts and tossed aside more and more letters, full of rather queer alarmist reports. So argued and acted the great Carthaginian Empire. That meaningless prejudice, the curse of commercial states, that stupidity is somehow practical and that genius is somehow futile, led them to starve and abandon that great artist in the school of arms, whom the gods had given them in vain.

Why do men entertain this queer idea that what is sordid must always overthrow what is magnanimous; that there is some dim connection between brains and brutality, or that it does not matter if a man is dull if he is also mean? Why do they vaguely think of all chivalry as sentiment and all sentiment as weakness? They do it because they are, like all men, primarily inspired by religion. For them, as for all men, the first fact is their notion of the nature of things; their idea about what world they are living in. And it is their faith that the only ultimate thing is fear and therefore that the very heart of the world is evil. They believe death is stronger than life, and therefore dead things must be stronger than living things; whether those dead things are gold and iron and machinery or rocks and rivers and forces of nature. It may sound fanciful to say that men we meet at tea-tables or talk with at garden-parties are secretly worshippers of Baal or Moloch. But this kind of commercial mind has its own cosmic vision, and it is the vision of Carthage. It has in it the brutal blunder of the ruin of Carthage. The Punic power fell because there is in this materialism a mad indifference to real thought. By disbelieving in the soul, it comes to disbelieving in the mind. Being too practical to be moral, it denies what every practical soldier calls the moral of an army. It fancies that money will fight when men will no longer fight. So it was with the Punic merchant princes. Their religion was a religion of despair, even when their practical fortunes were hopeful. How could they understand that the Romans could hope even when their fortunes were hopeless? Their religion was a religion of force and fear; how could they understand that men can still despise fear even when they submit to force? Their philosophy of the world had weariness in its very heart; above all they were weary of warfare; how should they understand those who still wage war even when they are weary of it? In a word, how should they understand the mind of man, who had so long bowed before mindless things, money and brute force and gods who had the hearts of beasts? They awoke suddenly to the news that the embers they had disdained too much even to tread out were flames again; that Hasdrubal was defeated, that Hannibal was outnumbered, that Scipio had carried the war into Spain; that he had carried it into Africa. Before the gates of the golden city Hannibal fought his last fight for it and lost, and Carthage fell as nothing has fallen since Satan. The name of the New City remains only as a name. There is no stone of it left on the sand. Another war was indeed waged before the final destruction: but the destruction was final. Only men digging in its deep foundation centuries after found a heap of hundreds of little skeletons, the holy relics of that religion. For

Carthage fell because she was faithful to her own philosophy and had carried to its logical conclusion her vision of the universe. Moloch had eaten his children.

The gods had risen again, and the demons had been defeated after all. But they had been defeated by the defeated, and almost defeated by the dead. Nobody understands the romance of Rome, and why she rose afterwards to a representative leadership that seemed almost fated and fundamentally natural. Who does not keep in mind the agony of horror and humiliation through which she had continued to testify to the sanity that is the soul of Europe? She came to stand alone amid an empire because she had once stood alone amid ruin and waste. After that all men knew in their hearts that she had been representative of mankind, even when she was rejected of men. And there fell on her the shadow from a shining and still invisible light and the burden of things to be. It is not for us to guess in what manner or moment the mercy of God might have rescued the world, but it is certain that the struggle which established Christendom would have been very different if there had been an empire of Carthage instead of an empire of Rome. We have to thank the patience of the Punic Wars if, in after ages, divine things descended at least upon human things and not inhuman. Europe evolved into its own vices and its own impotence... but the worst it evolved into was not like what it had escaped. Can any man in his senses compare the great wooden doll, which the children expected to eat a little of the dinner, with the great idol, which would have been expected to eat the children? That is the measure of how far the world went astray, compared to how far it might have gone astray. If the Romans were ruthless, they were so toward an enemy and not merely a rival. They remembered not trade routes and regulations, but the faces of sneering men, and they hated the hateful soul of Carthage... If, after all these ages, we are in some sense at peace with paganism, and can think more kindly of our fathers, it is well to remember what was and might have been. For this reason alone we can take lightly the load of antiquity and need not shudder at a nymph on a stone fountain or a cupid on a valentine. Laughter and sadness link us with things long past and remembered without dishonor, and we can see not altogether without tenderness the twilight sinking around the Sabine farm and hear the household gods rejoice when Catullus comes home to Sirmio. *Deleta est Carthago.*[102]

In 1991, something *directly contrary* to the historic victory of Rome over Carthage occurred. Plunged into dust more than two thousand years ago,

---

102 "Carthage is destroyed." The preceding passage is from *The Everlasting Man*, in *The Collected Works of G. K. Chesterton*, vol. 2, pp. 277–282. —Ed.

civilization took revenge. This time Rome fell (the Third Rome), and Carthage won a victory. The course of world history was reversed. All those cruel words that Chesterton directed against Carthage are perfectly applicable to those who won a victory in the "Cold War." *Mercantile civilization prevailed over a heroic, ascetic, and Spartan civilization.* The putrid spirit of plutocracy proved stronger than the perplexed and confused "Romans" of socialism, who had lost their vigilance. Significantly, Chesterton ties Rome's victory over Carthage to such events unique to Christianity as the birth of Christ in the Roman Empire, a land civilization. By this logic, only the Antichrist could have been born in a sea civilization.

The First Stage of the Collapse: The Weakening of Soviet Influence in the Global Leftist Movement

The collapse of the USSR proceeded in a few stages. The first stage was characterized by a weakening of the influence of the USSR in foreign countries: in Africa, Latin America, the Far East, and Western Europe (where, under the banner of "Eurocommunism," a reorientation of Leftist and Communist parties away from the Soviet Union to petty-bourgeois and specifically European political realities had begun). This had already begun in the 1970s and reached its apogee in the 1980s. In this period, the propaganda campaign against the denunciation of "Stalin's repressions" and the totalitarian Soviet regime reached its peak, and even Leftist political circles preferred to acquiesce in this criticism to remain politically correct. In the 1980s, especially after Gorbachev came to power, Moscow not only did not try to oppose something to these tendencies, but adopted them and began to gradually repeat the criticisms of Stalinism and, later, of Leninism, undermining the foundations of Soviet historical self-consciousness. Instead of strengthening its influence in the global Leftist movement according to its geopolitical interests, the USSR adopted those propaganda clichés that had been implanted into this movement by the pro-capitalist, bourgeois powers interested only in weakening the land civilization and strengthening the sea civilization.

The representatives of the Fourth International,[103] the Trotskyists, played a special role in this. Already being radical opponents of Stalin and his policy of building socialism in one country from the 1920s and 1930s, Trotskyites made the USSR their main enemy, and in this fight with the USSR they joined in solidarity with any powers they could, including those they considered their "class enemies." Hatred toward the USSR and Stalin became the main feature of Trotskyism and led many of its representatives to side with the liberal camp, and to join the ranks of the more consistent and radical Atlanticists.[104] These groups contributed heavily to tearing the international Left and, more importantly, the Communist movement, away from the USSR, beginning in the 1970s.

Because of these processes, the USSR's network of influence in countries outside direct Soviet control was undermined, weakened, and partially removed from the coordinating control of Moscow.

In other instances the same effect was produced by the inflexible policies of the USSR toward various ideological forces in the countries of the Third World (in particular, in Africa and the Islamic countries) where there was real opposition to American and Western European influence, but where no preconditions for a full-fledged socialist movement existed historically. One of the clear instances was Afghanistan, where the USSR made a bet only on the Communists, ignoring the many national and religious groups which, under different conditions, could have been allies of the USSR in their rejection of Americanism and liberal capitalism. Thus,

---

103 The Fourth International was established in Paris in 1938 to propagate the ideas of Trotsky and his followers in opposition to Stalinism. It still exists today.—Ed.

104 We see this in the fate of a political scientist like James Burnham and also, even more evidently, in the history of the ideological tendency of contemporary American neoconservatives, who evolved from radical Trotskyism to ultra-liberalism, imperialism, and undisguised capitalist hegemony.

toward the end of the 1980s, the outer zone of Soviet influence in the world began to gradually fall to pieces.

Geopolitically, this *undermined the global structure of the influence of the Heartland,* which in the epoch of the "Cold War" succeeded in transferring its fight with the civilization of the Sea to the periphery of the Eurasian mainland, or altogether beyond its borders.

The Second Stage of the Collapse: The End of the Warsaw Pact

Anti-Soviet "revolutions" in the countries of Eastern Europe, which culminated in the dissolution of the Warsaw Pact and *the liquidation of the socialist camp,* were the second stage. This was a colossal blow along the nearest zone of the USSR's strategic defenses. The loss of Eastern Europe was a nightmare that had haunted even Stalin and Beria, who had recognized the vulnerability of the structure of the European borders. The way Gorbachev's surrender of Eastern Europe proceeded was *the worst* possible scenario. Soviet troops were hastily removed from there, and, on a wave of anti-Sovietism, the vacated space was quickly filled by NATO troops, bourgeois ideology, and capitalist economics. *The Sea seized that which escaped from the control of the Land.* Carthage united to its zone of influence the territories from which Rome was expelled. Mackinder wrote, "Who rules East Europe commands the Heartland; who rules the Heartland commands the World-Island; who rules the World-Island commands the world."[105] After 1989, the "civilization of the sea" began to control Eastern Europe. Mackinder's project, inherited by the subsequent generation of Anglo-Saxon geopoliticians, all the way to Brzezinski, was put into practice.

Having lost Eastern Europe, the USSR lost its most important zone of defense and took a colossal geopolitical blow. What is more, this blow was not compensated by anything and was not justified by anything. The Soviet media of that period presented the events in Eastern Europe as the "victory of democracy," paralysing the will to self-preservation and healthy rational-

---

105 Halford Mackinder, *Democratic Ideals and Reality,* p. 106.

ity in the USSR itself: our obvious defeat was portrayed as the "victory of progress," and so forth. In this situation, the blame for which rests with Gorbachev and his circle, all the preconditions ripened for the final stage in this series of disasters, the dissolution of the USSR itself.

The Third Stage of the Collapse: the State Committee on the State of Emergency and the End of the USSR

This dissolution was evidently planned for June 1990, when the majority of Soviet Republics in the USSR, including the RSFSR, proclaimed their sovereignty. But if all other Soviet republics put autonomy from the center and the possibility of moving toward statehood into their concepts of sovereignty, the sovereignty of Russia had a more ambiguous meaning, as it proposed autonomy from the center of the government whose core was Russia. It meant Russia's declaration of liberation from itself. This gesture was based on a domestic policy struggle between the leadership of the RSFSR, led by Yeltsin, and the leadership of the USSR, led by Gorbachev. But the fate of the government itself was put at stake in this opposition.

By June 1991, it became clear that the process of granting autonomy to the Soviet republics was gaining momentum, and their leaders raised the question of signing a new Union treaty, which would have converted them into independent and sovereign governments. Using the formal mechanisms of the Constitution of the USSR, the heads of the Soviet republics, while deciding their domestic policy goals, strove to use the weakness and blindness of the Union's center for their own interests.

The summer of 1991 passed in preparation for the denouement. It came on August 19, 1991, when a group of high-ranking Soviet leaders — the Vice-President of the USSR, G. I. Yanayev; the Minister of Defense, D. T. Yazov; the Chairman of the KGB of the USSR, V. A. Kryuchkov; the Minister of Internal Affairs of the USSR, B. K. Pugo; the Prime Minister of the USSR, V. S. Pavlov, and others — executed a coup *for the prevention of the dissolution of the USSR*. This event entered history under the name of "the 1991 August Coup." Gorbachev was placed under house arrest at his Crimean dacha in Foros, where he was vacationing. The leadership of the RSFSR was put under siege in the Parliament (the "White House"). Geopolitically, the group that had performed the coup *was acting in the interests of the Heartland* and attempted to prevent the collapse of the USSR, which was becoming inevitable given the continuation of the policies of Gorbachev and his circle, and of Yeltsin, despite the quarrels between them. Gorbachev did not make any effective efforts to preserve the USSR, and Yeltsin did all he could to get his share of power in the country, risking its complete fragmentation. In other words, the actions of the conspirators were *geopolitically warranted and politically justified.* The series of catastrophes suffered by the Soviet ideology, government, and geopolitical system, and the absence of any effective policies of opposition whatsoever from the side of the legally designated power, forced them to take extreme measures. However, the high-ranking bureaucrats who had seized power lacked the spirit, mind, and will to bring the matter they had begun to its end; they wavered, fearing to take abrupt, repressive measures against their opponents, and lost. Three days after August 19, 1991, it became evident that the rebellion of the conservatives who had tried to save the USSR had failed. Gorbachev returned to Moscow, and the conspirators were arrested. But from then on, *de facto* power in the country and in its capital was transferred to Yeltsin and his circle, while Gorbachev's role remained nominal. To finally secure his successes in the struggle for power, only one thing remained for Yeltsin to do: dethrone Gorbachev once and for all. For that, it was necessary to dissolve the USSR itself.

The Białowieża Forest

Under the influence of his advisors (G. Burbulis, S. Shakhrai, S. Stankevich), Yeltsin went for this. On December 8, 1991, an agreement for the creation of a Commonwealth of Independent States was signed by the heads of the RSFSR, the Republic of Belarus, and Ukraine in the Białowieża Forest, which meant the end of the existence of the USSR as a unified government. Thus, another geopolitical zone, established throughout many centuries of Russian history around the core of the Heartland, was lost.

This event continued the series of earlier events and signified a radical "geopolitical catastrophe" (this expression for the characteristics of the events of 1991 was used by Putin). Without any opposition or geopolitical compensation whatsoever, the Soviet government was divided into seventeen independent governments, now lacking a single, supranational leadership. Thus, a government that had withstood so many serious shocks — from the yoke of the Time of Troubles to the Revolution of 1917 and the Civil War — ended its existence. If earlier Russia had also suffered territorial loses comparable to those which occurred in 1991, they were compensated for by acquisitions in other areas, or they lasted for only a short while. From the time of Gorbachev and Yeltsin we can observe an absolutely new historical stage, when the leadership of Russia not only stopped increasing its territory or its zones of influence, but reduced them, radically, on a large scale, and irreversibly. Every Czar or General Secretary had increased the space of the Heartland's influence. The first to deviate from this rule was Mikhail Gorbachev, and Boris Yeltsin continued his policies. The fabricated structure of the CIS was an instrument of "civilizational divorce," and did not carry even a hint of general leadership or potential for the integration of former republics.

This was how the second dream of Mackinder, who had proposed the separation of the territory of Russia into several governments, including those that were a result of Gorbachev's and Yeltsin's reforms, such as the Baltic countries (Latvia, Lithuania, Estonia), Belarus, Ukraine, Moldova, Armenia, Georgia, and Azerbaijan, was put into practice. Yugorussia and Dagestan (which included all the Northern Caucasus) had also figured on Mackinder's map. But in its main features, the thalassocratic project of the redistribution of Russia's structure in favor of the sea power was realized *by the hands of Russia's "democratic" leadership.*

It is significant that the victory of the civilization of the Sea was this time so convincing and deep that it was not only limited by the seizure of new strategic territories, which had been let out from the control of the civilization of Land and placed under the control of the civilization of the Sea (the countries of NATO). A "sea" ideology, or the influence of Carthage, had spread also to Russia itself, which accepted entirely *the system of values of the victors* in the "Cold War." *Geopolitical capitulation was accompanied by civilizational and ideological capitulation:* bourgeois democracy, liberalism, the market economy, parliamentarism, and the ideology of the rights of man were proclaimed to be the dominant principles of the "new Russia." Carthage penetrated the Heartland. And if we consider the deep significance that Chesterton had given to the outcome of the Punic Wars, the basis of all the historical generalizations of all geopoliticians, it is difficult to overestimate the importance of these geopolitical events. In this period, a colossal blow was brought upon the civilization of Land, the consequences of which have predetermined the general distribution of powers in the world *until today.*

The Unipolar Moment

The collapse of the USSR and the entire Soviet planetary geopolitical structure meant a cardinal change of the entire global map. This was the end of the Yalta system and *the conclusion of the bipolar world.* In such a situation the Heartland, as the core of the civilization of Land, ceased to be an equal participant (half) of the world system and drastically lost its former positions. Instead of a bipolar world, the era of a *unipolar* world began. The American analyst and specialist in the sphere of international relations, Charles Krauthammer, wrote in the influential American journal *Foreign Affairs*, "It has been assumed that the old bipolar world would beget a multipolar world with power dispersed to new centers in Japan,

Germany (and/or 'Europe'), China, and a diminished Soviet Union / Russia. . [...] All three of these assumptions are mistaken. The immediate post-Cold War world is not multipolar. It is unipolar. The center of world power is the unchallenged superpower, the United States, attended by its Western allies."[106]

The new architecture of international relations, *built on the sole dominance of the USA,* replaced the previous *bipolarity.* This meant, first, that the general structure of the bipolar world was preserved, but *one of the two poles simultaneously withdrew.* The socialist camp and its military-strategic expression, the Warsaw Pact, were disbanded at the end of the 1980s; in 1991 the Soviet Union was disbanded. But the capitalist camp, which rallied around the USA, the military NATO bloc, and the bourgeois-capitalist ideology (which dominated in the West) during the "Cold War," *was preserved in its entirety.* However the Soviet leaders in Gorbachev's era might have tried to present themselves as developing a new system of international relations "upholding the interests of the USSR," an impartial analysis shows unequivocally that the West defeated the East; the USA defeated the USSR; the capitalist system defeated the socialist one; the market economy defeated the planned economy.

In the Yalta world there were two supports for the architecture of international relations, alongside a complicated system of checks. In the new unipolar world only one authority remained: the USA and its allies. From now on, they acted both as prosecutor and judge, and even as the executor of punishment, in all contested questions of international life. NATO was not dissolved; on the contrary, the former countries of the socialist camp of Eastern Europe, and later also the Baltic countries, were integrated with it at an accelerated pace. NATO expanded to the East, and the failed socialist system was replaced not by some "third" alternative (for which the archi-

---

106 Charles Krauthammer, "The Unipolar Moment," *Foreign Affairs,* vol. 70, No. 1 (1990/1991), pp. 23–33.

tects of perestroika had hoped), but the classical, and at times coarse and brutal, "good old" capitalism.

The Geopolitics of the Unipolar World: Center-Periphery

The geopolitics of the unipolar world has one peculiarity. The West-East axis, which prevailed in the ideological confrontation of the era of the Yalta World, was replaced by the model of *Center-Periphery*. From now on, the USA and the countries of Western Europe (the members of NATO) were placed at the center of the world, and everyone else on the periphery. This symmetry of core/outskirts replaces the symmetry of two poles. The dualism of the Yalta World, concentrated and strictly formalized both geopolitically and ideologically, is replaced by more decentralized and heterogeneous rays, issuing from the core of unipolarity and extending to the global outskirts (earlier called the Third World). The victors of the "Cold War" are from now on placed at the center, and around them, in concentric circles, all the rest are distributed according to the degree of their strategic, political, economic, and cultural proximity to the center. The neighboring circle practically belongs to the center: Europe, the other countries of NATO, and Japan. Furthermore, the rapidly developing capitalist, democratic countries are allies of the USA, or at least neutral. Finally, at a distant orbit are the weakly developed countries undergoing the first stage of modernization and Westernization, preserving definite archaic traits, but frequently possessing a stagnant economy and a rudimentary or "illiberal" democracy. This geometrical configuration of the world took shape in the 1990s to replace the Yalta system.

In his book *The Triumph of the West*, J. M. Roberts wrote the following about this: "[T]he 'success' of our [Western, American—AD] civilisation does not have to be discussed in such [i.e., moral—Tr.] terms. It is a matter of simple historical effectiveness. Almost all the master principles and ideas now reshaping the modern world emanate from the West; they have spread round the globe and other civilizations have crumbled before them. To acknowledge that, by itself, tells us nothing about whether the outcome is good or bad, admirable or deplorable. It only registers that this is the age of the first world civilisation and it is the civilisation of the West."[107]

And then: "I doubt whether an abstraction so general as 'civilisation' can meaningfully have words like 'good' and 'bad' attached to it. It remains true that western civilization has knowingly and unknowingly forced other civilisations to concessions such as they had never before had to make to any external force."[108] It is important in Roberts' work that he tries to separate *the fact from its moral evaluation*. Western civilization, meaning bourgeois liberal ideology, its value system, and the related set of sociopolitical norms (parliamentary democracy, the free market, human rights, the separation of powers, the independence of the press, etc.) defeated *all civilizational alternatives* on a planetary scale. Just as only one of two geopolitical poles survived via a modification of the opposition along the symmetry of West-East according to the model of Center-Periphery, in the sphere of ideology, instead of two competing paradigmatic and sociopolitical systems there remained *only one,* which acquired global scope. Ideologically, this can be formulated thus: liberal democracy (the paradigmatic core) and everything else (the paradigmatic periphery).

The Geopolitics of the Neoconservatives

The victory of the West in the "Cold War," which resulted in unipolarity and the triumph of Western civilization, was interpreted in different ways in the USA itself. We encounter one kind of interpretation in the ideological movement of the American neoconservatives, followers of the philosopher Leo Strauss, thought of in the USA as a far-Right school of con-

---

107 J. M. Roberts, *The Triumph of the West: The Origin, Rise, and Legacy of Western Civilization* (Boston: Little Brown, 1985), p. 41.

108 Ibid.

servatism.[109] The neoconservatives reasoned in terms of "force," "enemy," "domination," and so on. But this means that, according to their view, to maintain control over society, an external threat is always needed. With the disintegration of the Soviet Union, it was necessary to replace it with another. This became Islam. The neoconservatives have called for an increase in America's military budget "for the defense of America's role as the global fulcrum." The theory of American primacy leaves no opportunities for a multipolar world. Through the durable establishment of its own laws far and wide, a dominant power can preserve its ruling position over the world. This is called "global hegemony," which the neoconservatives themselves propose to call a "benevolent hegemony."[110]

The neoconservatives first became an influential force in American political life in the 1980s, and their influence peaked after the election of George W. Bush in 2000. The neoconservatives interpreted this unipolar moment in terms of "empire." From their point of view, the USA proceeded systematically throughout its history toward global hegemony, and when the last global competitor (the USSR, and the socialist camp with it) fell, it attained its initial goal and logically took the reins of world government. In August 1996, neoconservatives Kristol and Kagan[111] published an article in *Foreign Affairs,* in which they wrote: "Today when the evil empire is perhaps already defeated, American must strive to carry out the best American leadership, inasmuch as earlier America did not have such a golden chance to spread democracy and the free market beyond its borders. America's earlier position was not as good as it is today. Thus, the corresponding goal of

---

109 Shadia B. Drury, *Leo Strauss and the American Right* (London: Palgrave Macmillan, 1999).

110 Gary Dorrien, "Benevolent Global Hegemony: William Kristol and the Politics of American Empire," *Logos* vol. 3, No. 2 (2004).

111 William Kristol (b. 1952) is one of the leading American neoconservatives, being the founder of the neoconservative journal, The Weekly Standard, and co-founder of the Project for the New American Century, which was the leading neoconservative think tank between 1997 and 2006. Robert Kagan (b. 1958) was also co-founder of the Project, and is a member of the Council on Foreign Relations.—Ed.

the United States must be the defense of this superiority to the best of its powers and over the longest period possible."[112]

One of the other theorists of neoconservatism, Laurence Vance, wrote concerning this idea, "Nothing, however, compares to the U.S. global empire. What makes U.S. hegemony unique is that it consists, not of control over great land masses or population centers, but of a global presence unlike that of any other country in history. [...] The U. S. global empire — an empire that Alexander the Great, Caesar Augustus, Genghis Khan, Suleiman the Magnificent, Justinian, and King George V would be proud of."[113] This understanding of the new architecture of the world and of the system of international relations in terms of a global American empire could not fail to influence the methods by which America's strategic plans were implemented. Intoxicated by victory, the Americans began at times to conduct themselves unceremoniously. The neoconservatives openly praised American hegemony.[114] They elevated the liberal-capitalist ideology to the status of an *indisputable dogma*, and they proclaimed American supremacy and the American empire to be the ideal political system and the optimal arrangement of the new system of international relations.

The neoconservatives imparted a rather aggressive style to American policy in the 1990s. In identifying the national interests of the USA with "the good" for all humanity, they provoked strong opposition and a wave of protests both in America[115] and in other parts of the world.

---

112 William Kristol and Robert Kagan, "Toward a Neo-Reaganite Foreign Policy," *Foreign Affairs* vol. 75, No. 4 (1996), pp. 18–32. [The quote in Dugin's text does not match the original English text exactly, but is more of a summary of the spirit of the argument.—Tr.]

113 Laurence Vance, "The Burden of Empire," available at www.informationclearinghouse.info/article5876.htm.

114 Kristol and Kagan, "Toward a Neo-Reaganite Foreign Policy."

115 Shadia B. Drury, *Leo Strauss and the American Right*.

The Kozyrev Doctrine

The sudden collapse of the Soviet system and the penetration of the influence of thalassocracy deep into Russia itself exerted a colossal influence upon the structure of the world. In the first years of Boris Yeltsin's administration (1991–1993), all political processes inside the Russian Federation proceeded in the thalassocratic spirit. In that period, the so-called "Kozyrev Doctrine" was maintained in foreign policy, named after Yeltsin's Minster of Foreign Affairs.

The "Kozyrev Doctrine" held that unipolarity was *an accomplished fact*, that the dominance of the USA in the world should be recognized as a given, and that under such conditions only one thing remained for Russia (as the most important of the post-Soviet nations) to do: to integrate itself with the West-centric world by attaining a position of as much influence and importance as possible, to the maximum extent that the economic, strategic, and social resources of the Russian Federation could permit. This recognition was accompanied by the *moral* approval of the end of the bipolar world and by a resolute *condemnation* of the preceding bipolarity and of the entire ideology, policy, and geopolitics of the Soviet period. Kozyrev admitted: in the "Cold War" the West did not merely win by force, having proved more stable and powerful; it was also historically *right*. After that, it remained for Russia only to recognize this right of the victor and to join in solidarity with him, both in business and in morals.

In practice, this meant *the recognition of the legitimacy of the American vision of the world and consent to build Russia's foreign policy in correspondence with the general strategic policy of the USA,* adapting to it and only then pursuing its own national interests. Kozyrev accepted the rules of the game of the unipolar world as *proper,* and proceeded from this assumption when establishing the priorities and goals of Russia's foreign policy.

In relation to the post-Soviet space, this entailed Moscow's renunciation of any efforts whatsoever to reestablish its influence in neighboring countries, to move to a bipolar dynamic of relations with them, and to support the individual movements of the CIS countries toward gradual integration with the West and globalization. Such an attitude toward the USA and the West, which held sway in Russia in the early 1990s, meant direct *capitulation* before the adversary and the recognition of his right and his victory, both factually and morally. In a certain sense, this meant the start of the establishment of *foreign control of the country* by the representatives of the pole that had become global. In the first Yeltsin administration, Prime Minister Yegor Gaidar[116] formed a group of economic reformers, in which Anatoly Chubais[117] played an active role, who were led by a group of American experts under the leadership of Jeffrey Sachs.[118] They insisted on shock therapy and the accelerated transfer of Russia's entire economy to the ultraliberal railway. This led to catastrophic consequences: the impoverishment of the population, the devaluation of the economy, the complete decline of industry, the privatization of basic profitable enterprises, and the rise of new oligarchs who had seized key positions in the country by illegal means.

Geopolitically, this period can be thought of as *the flooding of the Land,* or the establishment of direct control over the Heartland by the sea power. This was a time of unprecedented success for the Atlanticists; they had not only surrounded Russia with a dense ring of states loyal to the civilization of the Sea, they had also penetrated deep inside the country, spreading their networks to encompass the majority of the significant administrative,

116 Yegor Gaidar (1956–2009) was Acting Prime Minister of Russia during the second half of 1992, and was the leader of many of the economic reforms which rapidly transitioned Russia away from Communism ('shock therapy'). He was held responsible by many Russians for the economic hardships of the 1990s.—Ed.

117 Anatoly Chubais (b. 1955) is a Russian economist who spearheaded the privatisation of the Russian economy in the early 1990s.—Ed.

118 M. N. Poltoranin, *Authority as an Explosive: The Heritage of Czar Boris* (Moscow: Eksmo, 2010).

political, economic, media, informational, and even military structures, which had either been corrupted by the new oligarchs or directly infiltrated by Atlanticist agents of influence with the approval of the democratic reformers then in power.

The Contours of Russia's Collapse

Yeltsin came to power on a wave of attempts by various administrative groups in Russia itself to achieve autonomy. Thus, the former autonomous republics automatically received the status of national republics after the RSFSR's declaration of sovereignty, and they hurried to add a clause about their sovereignty to their constitutions, repeating the logic of the USSR and obviously expecting in the final stages to declare their exit from the composition of Russia as soon as a good opportunity presented itself. In his battle with Gorbachev and his attempt to seize and secure power, Yeltsin not only reacted favorably to this, but also actively contributed to this process. His statement made in Ufa on August 6, 1990, entered history: "Take as much sovereignty as you can swallow." This was unambiguously clear, and already from the 1990s the national republics in the composition of the RSFSR, and later the Russian Federation, started to hastily give their declared sovereignty real meaning. Essentially, a stormy *construction of autonomous national statehood* began, with all its characteristic signs: one's own national language, an educational program, economic independence, political autonomy, and so on. A few republics prescribed norms in their constitutions that, besides sovereignty, contained all the attributes of an independent government. This was the case with Tartarstan, Bashkiria, Komi, Yakutia (Sakha), Chechnya, and so on. In particular, in the Constitution of the Republic of Sakha, adopted on April 27, 1992, this Republic was declared "a sovereign, democratic, and juridical government, founded on a

narod's right to self-determination." The Constitution included all the attributes of a sovereign government: a national language, the introduction
of a national currency, a treasury supplying its negotiability, and its own
army; it also established a visa requirement for citizens of other republics in
the Russian Federation. The constitutions of a few other republics were put
together in the same spirit.

The general tendency from the end of the 1990s consisted in the continuation of the growing extent of this declared sovereignty and the insis-
tence that the federal center respect it.

The national policy of the Russian Federation was put together in
this spirit. Its contours were established by Ramzan Abdulatipov,[119] Valery
Tishkov,[120] and others, who justified the need for a gradual transition
from a federal system to a confederation and then to a complete separation of the national republics (or, at least, a few of them) into independent
governments.

Thus, the last part of Mackinder's plan concerning the partition of
Russia, proposing the separation of the Northern Caucasus (Dagestan) and
Yugorussia, became entirely realistic in this period.

Mackinder also called Eastern Siberia "Lenaland" and did not exclude
the possibility of its eventual integration with the USA's sphere of influence.[121] He also mentioned in passing the creation of a few independent
governments in the Volga region. Later, Zbigniew Brzezinski outlined
analogous plans for the dismemberment of Russia in his works published
in *Foreign Affairs*.[122] After the collapse of the outer regions of the Heartland

---

119 Ramzan Abdulatipov, *The Science of Federalism [Federology]*, (Saint Petersburg: Pitr, 2004).
(Abdulatipov [b. 1946] is a Dagestani who was Chairman of the Chamber of Nationalities
of the RSFSR from 1990 until 1993. Since 2013 he has been Head of the Republic of
Dagestan.—Ed.)

120 Valery Tishkov (b. 1941) is a Russian ethnologist who was the chairman of the State
Committee of the RSFSR on nationalities in 1992.—Ed.

121 Halford Mackinder, 'The Round World and the Winning of the Peace,' *Foreign Affairs* 21
(1943), pp. 595–605.

122 Zbigniew Brzezinski, "A Geostrategy for Eurasia," in *Foreign Affairs* (September/October
1997).

at the start of the 1990s, it became evident that it was then the Russian Federation's turn. Moreover, the representatives of the reformer democrats then in power had a favorable attitude toward these processes on the whole, drawing up even their domestic policies in accordance with the interests of the civilization of the Sea.

The Establishment of a Russian School of Geopolitics

After 1991 and the end of the USSR, a Russian school of geopolitics began to develop in Russia. The first geopolitical texts ("Continent Russia," "*The Subconsciousness of Eurasia*," etc.) were published.[123] In the newspaper *Day*, the article "The Great War of Continents" was published, where the principles of the geopolitical method were set forth in journalistic form. Beginning in 1992, the theoretical journal *Elements* was published regularly. It contained a section entitled "Geopolitical Notebooks" and made available the works of classical geopoliticians and more topical geopolitical commentaries. Thus, a fully-fledged *Russian geopolitical school of a neo-Eurasianist orientation* took shape, continuing the traditions of the Slavophiles, Eurasianists, and other Russian geopoliticians, but also taking into account the significant groundwork made in this discipline throughout the twentieth century in the Anglo-Saxon and German schools, and also in France in the 1970s (the school of Yves Lacoste).[124]

In this same period, the prominent European geopoliticians Jean Thiriart, Alain de Benoist, Robert Steuckers, Carlo Terracciano, Claudio Mutti, and others visited Russia, delivering lectures and seminars and familiarizing the Russian public with the principles of the geopolitical method and its terminology. The historical situation allowed for the summarization of historical experience in the development of this discipline and for the laying down of the foundations of a fully-fledged geopolitical

---

123 Alexander Dugin, *The Mysteries of Eurasia* (Moscow: Arctogaia, 1991), Chapters 1 and 2.

124 Yves Lacoste (b. 1929) has written many works pertaining to geopolitics, and is the head of the French Institute for Geopolitics.—Ed.

school. In the early 1990s, instruction in geopolitics began at the Military Academy of the General Staff of the Russian Federation (under the instructions of the future Minister of Defense, I. Rodionov, in the Department of Strategy, then led by Lieutenant General H. P. Kolokotov),[125] where its principal ideas were also formed and published somewhat later in the textbook, *Foundations of Geopolitics*.[126]

By 1993, the basic notions of geopolitics and Eurasianism became well-known to a certain circle of political scientists, strategists, and military analysts, and later the significance of the geopolitical analysis of unfolding events became an integral part of the interpretation of the historical moment in which Russia found itself. The specific character of the geopolitical method is responsible for the fact that this discipline was first disseminated in patriotic circles which opposed the regime of Yeltsin and the "Young Reformers," which gave it a certain political orientation. Incidentally, it was this perspective that all previous generations of geopoliticians, formulating their views concurrently with their active participation in the depths of historical processes, never departed from and did not try to leave.

Thus, the neo-Eurasianists, who had gathered around the journal *Elements* and the newspaper *Day*, became the ideological inspiration behind the unification of the diverse forces of Rightists, Leftists, and nationalists against Yeltsin and his ultraliberal, Atlanticist circle on geopolitical grounds.

The Geopolitics of the Political Crises of October 1993

The Russian leadership was distinctly divided by 1993. Part of the political leadership moved to become Yeltsin's opposition, in particular Vice President A. Rutskoy, as well as the head of the Supreme Soviet of the RSFSR, R. Khasbulatov, and the majority of the deputies who had been

125 N. P. Kolokotov and N. G. Popov, *Problems of Strategy and of the Operative Art* (Moscow: The Military Academy of the General Staff of the Armed Forces, 1993).

126 Alexander Dugin, *Foundations of Geopolitics*.

supporters of Yeltsin in 1991, but who had been disappointed by his later policies. This division, besides emerging from personal conflicts among some of those involved, also had some geopolitical basis. Around Yeltsin was a core of advisors from the group of Young Reformers of an ultraliberal orientation (Y. Gaidar, A. Chubais, B. Nemtsov, I. Khakamada, A. Kozyrev, etc.) and oligarchs (B. Berezovsky, V. Gusinsky, etc.). They urged Yeltsin toward closer relations with the USA and the West, toward the development of Atlanticist geopolitics, and toward complete compliance with the directives coming from the civilization of the Sea. In foreign policy, this was expressed in unconditional support for all American undertakings ("the Kozyrev doctrine"). In economics there was the implementation of ultraliberal reforms and monetarism (Y. Gaidar, A. Chubais). Domestically, it occurred as democratization, Westernization, and the liquidation of socialist and socially-oriented institutions. In the question of the national republics, it had a favorable attitude toward the strengthening of their sovereignty. In all senses, the core that had rallied around Yeltsin and was urging him to continue moving in this direction was marked by the whole set of features of geopolitical Atlanticism, and was a striking representative of thalassocracy both in politics (domestic and foreign) and in the sphere of paradigmatic values. The general model of Yeltsin's rule was oligarchical and represented the interests of a few influential oligarchical clans, who had argued among themselves for influence over a short-sighted "democratic monarch," who swiftly ruined himself with drink and badly misunderstood the situation. In this manner, the 1993 crisis had a geopolitical focus: on Yeltsin's side were the agents of influence of the civilization of the Sea; on the side of the opposition (the Supreme Soviet) were the supporters of the civilization of Land.

The most dramatic moments of this confrontation in domestic politics were the events of September and October 1993, which ended in the shelling of the Supreme Soviet by military units entrusted to Yeltsin on October 4. Essentially, this was a brief flash of *civil war*, where two geopolitical forces collided: the supporters of the civilization of the Sea and foreign domination and the supporters of the civilization of Land, the restoration of Russia's sovereignty, the preservation of its integrity, and a return to the tellurocratic model of values (the supporters of the Supreme Soviet). As is well-known, the former triumphed over the latter. In the course of dramatic opposition and bitter resistance, the armed forces, under Yeltsin's control, took the building of the Supreme Soviet by storm, crushed the power of its defenders, and dismantled the Parliament, arresting all the leading personalities of the opposition.

Yeltsin's adversaries represented various political and ideological tendencies: both Left-Communist and Right-nationalist, and there was also a significant flank of democrats disappointed in Yeltsin. They were all united by a rejection of the general thrust of policy and, correspondingly, Atlanticism. The newspaper *Day* became the opposition's ideological center, published by the patriotic publicist Alexander Prokhanov. It is revealing that in one way or another all the most significant figures of the anti-Yeltsin opposition spoke out in favor of Eurasianism in 1993: R. Khasbulatov, the Chairman of the Constitutional Court, V. Zorkin, and Vice President A. Rutskoy, to say nothing of Yeltsin's more radical opponents: Communists, nationalists, and supporters of Orthodox monarchy.

The Change in Yeltsin's Views after the Conflict with Parliament

After this outcome, a decisive victory for Yeltsin and his circle, measures were taken to impart a degree of legitimacy to the consequences of the upheaval. A constitution copied from Western models was hastily adopted, and elections were conducted under the strict supervision of the authorities in the State Duma. But despite their efforts, the authorities did not receive much support from the population, which gave its voice to a populist, Vladimir Zhirinovsky,[127] who espoused nationalist and patriotic rhetoric, and to the even more oppositional anti-liberal leader of the Communist Party of the Russian Federation, Gennady Zyuganov.[128] The position of Yeltsin and his supporters was then such that, theoretically, they could have carried out whatever policy they wished, including being done with the opposition and its leaders once and for all, since it had suffered a crushing defeat and lost the will to resistance (and they had been arrested or had squandered the faith of their supporters). Although the opposition once again had a majority in the elected Duma, the new Constitution, which had secured the model of a presidential republic and given extraordinary powers to the President, allowed the ruling authorities to implement practically any policy without having to reckon with anything.

At that moment, however, Yeltsin made a decision, the meaning of which was *not to force the issue of previous Atlanticist policies*, nor to finish off the opposition (its leaders were soon released under an amnesty), but to correct the pro-Western course, while putting the brakes on Russia's collapse. It is difficult to say with certainty what inspired this decision. It is possible that one of the factors was the stronger influence of powerful actors close to Yeltsin (A. Korzhakov, M. Barsukov, etc.) whose significance grew in the critical period of the military operation against the Parliament in October 1993, and who differed subjectively in their vaguely patriotic

---

127 Vladimir Zhirinovsky (b. 1946) is the leader of the Liberal-Democratic Party of Russia, which he founded in 1990 as one of the first opposition parties allowed in the Soviet Union. An extreme nationalist of the populist variety, Zhirinovsky has long been known for his provocative statements and outrageous actions, which resonate with the frustrations of some Russian voters.—Ed.

128 Gennady Zyuganov (b. 1944) has been the First Secretary of the Communist Party of the Russian Federation (CPRF) since its foundation. The CPRF was founded in 1993 as a successor to the banned Communist Party of the USSR. It has attempted to formulate a new form of Communism with a more nationalist bent.—Ed.

worldviews (rather widespread among the Russian special services by a tradition rooted in the history of the USSR). In any case, after his victory over the opposition, Yeltsin decided to correct his reforms. The personnel changes were highly significant: instead of the ultraliberal Westernizer Y. Gaidar, he appointed the pragmatic "red director" V. Chernomyrdin;[129] instead of the Atlanticist A. Kozyrev, the moderate "patriot" and cautious "Eurasian" Y. Primakov, a specialist on the East and a foreign intelligence official.

The "Primakov Doctrine," as opposed to the "Kozyrev Doctrine," consisted of trying to defend Russia's national interests within the limits of what was possible under the conditions of the unipolar world, and also preserving ties with traditional allies and slipping out from under the control of the American diktat. This was a serious contrast in comparison to Kozyrev's unambiguously Atlanticist position.

All this, however, did not mean that Yeltsin rejected his former course entirely. It continued, and many key figures who were responsible for the execution of the Atlanticist line in Russian politics remained in their positions and retained their influence; additionally, significant levers of power were kept in the hands of oligarchs. But the rhythm of the Atlanticist reforms slowed substantially. Yeltsin began to brake reforms in this vein.

The critical moment was the Chechen campaign.

The First Chechen Campaign

In the framework of the general process of the sovereignization of the national republics in the early 1990s, various nationalist movements arose in Chechen-Ingush, one of which was the "All-National Congress of the Chechen People" created in 1990, having as its goal Chechnya's exit from the composition of the USSR and the establishment of an independent Chechen state. A former general of the Soviet Air Forces, Dzhokhar

---

129 Viktor Chernomyrdin (1938–2010) founded Gazprom, which is the state-owned natural gas company, and was Deputy Prime Minister for energy resources from 1992 until 1998.—Ed.

Dudayev, was its head. On June 8, 1991, at the second session, Dudayev, the national leader of the Chechen Republic, proclaimed the independence of the Chechen Republic of Ichkeria. After the defeat of the State Committee on the State of Emergency,[130] Dudayev and his supporters seized the building of the Supreme Soviet of Chechnya, and after the fall of the USSR, Dudayev announced that Chechnya was seceding from the Russian Federation. The separatists held an election, which Dudayev won, but Moscow did not recognize them. At that point what was essentially an armed confrontation began, and the separatists sped up the creation of their own armed forces. At the same time, in the spirit of the general orientation of the democratic reformers in favor of the acquisition of sovereignty, strange things began to happen: in June 1992 the Minister of Defense of the Russian Federation, Pavel Grachev, gave orders to give half the arms and ammunition in the Republic to the supporters of Dudayev. We cannot exclude the possibility of corruption, which would have been quite in the spirit of the economic and social processes of that time.

The victory of the separatists in Grozny led to the collapse of the Chechen-Ingush Autonomous Soviet Socialist Republic and to the declaration of a separate Ingushetian Republic within the structure of Russia. In that period, Chechnya became *de facto* independent, but *de jure* it was a government not recognized by any country. The Republic had the symbols of statehood (a flag, a coat of arms, a hymn) and the organs of power (a president, parliament, and lay courts). Even after this, when Dudayev stopped paying taxes into the general budget of the Federation and forbade employees of the Russian Special Services entry into the Republic, the federal center continued to transfer funds from the budget to Chechnya. In 1993, 11.5 billion roubles were earmarked for Chechnya. Russian oil continued to enter Chechnya until 1994, but it was not paid for and was resold abroad. These processes fit very well into the logic of the early 1990s.

---

130 This was the name that the officials who led the coup attempt against Gorbachev in August 1991 used for their group.—Ed.

Preparation by one of the republics for the exit from Russia correspond-
ed to the plan of the Atlanticists and those under their influence in the
Russian leadership, and explained the fact that many political powers and
influential media outlets (belonging to the oligarchs) in effect either closed
their eyes to what was happening or supported the actions of the Chechen
regime as a precedent for the other national republics. Thus, the last part of
Mackinder's plan, the fragmentation of Russia and the creation of a state in
the Northern Caucasus independent of Moscow, began to be implemented. This also aroused the support of Chechen separatists by the West and a
group of pro-Western regimes in the Arab world. Beginning in the summer
of 1994, combat operations began between troops loyal to Dudayev and
forces of the oppositional Provisional Council of the Chechen Republic,
which had taken a pro-Russian position. By winter it became clear that the
opposition did not have the strength to cope with the separatists, and on
December 1 the Russian Air Forces struck the airfields of Kalinovskaya and
Khankala and put all the aircraft under the control of the separatists out
of operation. On December 11, 1994, Yeltsin signed Decree No. 2169, "On
Measures to Ensure Law, Order and General Security in the Territories of
the Chechen Republic." The introduction of federal troops began after this.
In the first weeks of the war, Russian troops were able to occupy the northern regions of Chechnya practically without resistance. On December 31,
1994, the assault on Grozny began. It resulted in colossal losses for the federal forces and lasted not just a few days, as had been planned, but a few
months; only on March 6, 1995, did a troop of Chechen militants under the
command of Shamil Basayev[131] retreat from Chernorech'ye, the last region
of Grozny still controlled by the separatists. Only then did the city finally
come under the control of Russian forces.

---

131 Shamil Basayev (1965–2006) was the leader of the radical Islamist faction of the Chechen
guerrillas. He fought in both Chechen wars, and also fought against the Georgian government in the early 1990s.—Ed.

After the assault on Grozny, the main task for the Russian troops became the establishment of control over the flatland regions of the rebellious republic. By April 1995, the troops occupied almost the entire flatland territory of Chechnya, and the separatists resorted to subversive guerrilla operations.

On June 14, 1995, a group of 195 Chechen fighters under Shamil Basayev's command drove into the territory of the Stavropol Krai by truck and occupied the hospital in Budyonnovsk, taking hostages. After this terrorist act, the first round of talks took place in Grozny from June 19 to 22 between the Russian Federation and the separatists, at which an agreement was reached for a moratorium on military operations for an indefinite period. Overall, however, it was not observed. On January 9, 1996, a contingent of 256 fighters under the command of Salman Raduyev, Turpal-Ali Atgeriyev, and Khunkar-Pasha Israpilov executed a raid on the city of Kizlyar, where terrorists obliterated a group of military targets, and then seized the hospital and maternity home.

On March 6, 1996, a few contingents of fighters attacked Grozny from various directions, as it was still controlled by Russian troops, but were unable to take it. On April 21, 1996, federal troops were successful in eliminating Dzhokhar Dudayev in a missile attack.

On August 6, 1996, contingents of Chechen separatists again attacked Grozny. This time the Russian garrison could not hold the city. Simultaneously with the assault on Grozny, separatists also seized the cities of Gudermes and Argun.

On August 31, 1996, truce agreements were signed in the city of Khasavyurt by the representatives of Russia (Alexander Lebed, the Chairman of the Security Council) and Ichkeria (Aslan Maskhadov). On the basis of these agreements, all Russian troops were withdrawn from Chechnya, and the determination of the Republic's status was postponed until December 31, 2001. Essentially, this was *the capitulation of Moscow before the separatists*. The federal authority painted the picture that it could not resolve the situation by force and that it was compelled to follow the insurgents' lead.

From the moment the Khasavyurt Accord was concluded to the start of the Second Chechen War in 1999, Chechnya existed as a practically autonomous government, not directed from Moscow, for a second time.

It is important to emphasize that the most consistent liberal-democratic forces in Russia itself and the media under their control occupied an ambiguous position during the Chechen campaign, often depicting the separatists in a positive light as "freedom fighters" and the federal troops as "Russian colonialists." Corrupt bureaucrats, certain commanders, and oligarchic clans worked closely with the separatists and the criminal network of the Chechen diaspora in Russia itself to extract material and financial gain from the bloody tragedies. Quite often this brought irreparable damage to the military operations. At any moment, an order could come from above to stop a successful operation when it was becoming dangerous for the fighters. At the same time, the West rendered active political and social support to the separatists. Mercenaries from the Arab countries who came to Chechnya, as later became clear, were working for the CIA or British MI6.[132]

From a geopolitical point of view, this is entirely natural: the secession of Chechnya and the rise of a government independent from Moscow would have signified a move into the final stage of the Atlanticist plan for the fragmentation of Russia and the formation of new, independent governments on its territory (along the model of the collapse of the USSR). Chechnya was the acid test for all other potential separatists. And the fate of Russia — or more precisely, what was left of it — depended entirely on the fate of the Chechen campaign. From the fact that the Chechen campaign began at all, we see the vague will of Yeltsin not to allow Russia's disinte-

---

132 Aukai Collins, *My Jihad: The True Story of an American Mujahid's Amazing Journey from Usama Bin Laden's Training Camps to Counterterrorism with the FBI and CIA* (Guilford, CT: Lyons Press, 2002).

gration. And although this campaign was led very badly, irresolutely, and without forethought, with enormous and often futile losses on both sides, the fact that Moscow resisted Russia's disintegration had a tremendous significance. At that moment, many of Yeltsin's supporters from the camp of the Atlanticists moved into his opposition, being dissatisfied that he was not carrying out the general plan of the civilization of the Sea, or, at least, was slowing its realization. By 1996, this opposition became rather influential, and only the efforts of the well-known political engineer S. Kurginyan, working closely with B. Berezovsky and V. Gusinsky, led to the result that the oligarchs concluded a pact between themselves for the "conditional" support of Yeltsin in the elections. This was because of their fear of the possible and, under the conditions of the time, probable victory of the candidate of the Communist Party of the Russian Federation, Zyuganov. This phenomenon is known as "The Reign of the Seven Bankers"[133] by an analogy with the "Reign of the Seven Boyars," an epoch of the Russian Time of Troubles at the start of the seventeenth century. In any event, Yeltsin did not side with the Atlanticists entirely. But on the eve of the 1996 presidential elections, Yeltsin made a new sharp turn, discharging the patriotic members of the top brass from their posts (A. Korzhakov, M. Barsukov, etc.), and promoted the Atlanticist and ultraliberal A. Chubais. As a result of this demarche, the Khasavyurt Accord was soon concluded, which rendered all the losses suffered during the years of the First Chechen War null and put the situation back to the way it had been before the war. The separatists again came to control Grozny and most of Chechnya, which had been won by federal troops with such effort and with so much blood. Afterwards, they had every reason to expect that, under pressure from the

---

133 This was Boris Berezovsky (LogoVaz), Mikhail Khodorkovsky (Rosprom Group, Menatep), Mikhail Fridman (Alfa Group), Pyotr Aven (Alfa Group), Vladimir Gusinsky (Most Group), Vladimir Potanin (UNEXIM Bank), and Alexander Smolensky (SBS-Agro, Bank Stolichny). The term "Reign of the Seven Bankers" [смибанкирщина] was coined by the journalist A. Fadin. A. Fadin, "The Reign of the Seven Bankers as a New-Russian Variant of the Reign of the Seven Boyars," in *General Newspaper*, November 14, 1996.

West, Moscow would eventually be compelled to recognize the independence of the rebellious Republic. This would have meant the end of Russia.

The Geopolitical Outcomes of the Yeltsin Administration

We will briefly describe the main geopolitical outcomes of the reign of Boris Yeltsin, the first President of the Russian Federation. Overall, they can be characterized as the ruin of national interests; significant weakening of the country; surrender of strategic positions; direct pandering to the accelerated establishment of foreign rule over Russia; and destructive reforms in the economy, the results of which were the impoverishment of the population, the appearance of a new class of oligarchs, corrupt officials and their social service staff, and the destruction of the entire social infrastructure of society. This period can be compared only with the blackest cycles of Russian history: with the peak of the appanage fragmentation preceding the Mongolian conquests,[134] with the Time of Troubles, with the occupation of Rus by Polish and Swedish armies, and with the events of 1917, which led to the collapse of the Russian Empire and the Civil War. And as always, just as in these similar circumstances, *a geopolitical orientation to the West* prevailed, with the establishment of *an oligarchic regime* founded on the supposed omnipotence of competing groups in the political elite. However, Russia's losses during the Yeltsin administration — territorial losses (the fall of the USSR), the social and industrial catastrophe, the coming to power of corrupt, criminal elements and agents of American influence — all this was unprecedented and unheard of in its scale and duration, and the passive reaction of the population to it. *The 1990s were a monstrous geopolitical catastrophe for Russia.* Russian was transformed from a pole of the bipolar world and the civilization of Land, spreading its influence over

---

134 In the eleventh century, an appanage system was established in Kievan Rus, in which power was transferred to the eldest member of the royal dynasty rather than from father to son, This led to a great deal of infighting over the next four centuries, which led to the fragmentation and weakening of the state, and culminated in the invasion of Russia by the Mongols.—Ed.

half the planet into corrupt, disintegrating, second-rate state, swiftly losing its authority in the international arena and verging on collapse.

Of course, we cannot blame Yeltsin alone for this. His course was prepared by Gorbachev and his reforms and by a broad group of pro-Western agents of influence, supporters of liberal reforms, or simply by very incompetent, corrupt, and ignorant actors. But you also cannot absolve him from blame. Without this personality, who was only dimly aware of the true significance of the events that had unfolded around him and hardly understood what he himself was doing and where he was heading, it is doubtful whether the reformers could have done their destructive, subversive actions so successfully, dealing the country such a colossal blow.

After the shelling of the Supreme Soviet in October 1993, Yeltsin still made a certain correction in the general logic of his rule; he did not set out to destroy the opposition and slightly softened his destructive and suicidal policy, introducing a set of patriotic features into it. The fact that he ordered the Chechen campaign and did not accept Dudayev's ultimatum unconditionally, despite the urgings of the liberals and Atlanticists in his circle, already indicates that he preserved some residual view of the value of the territorial integrity of the government. In this he relied on his intuition; we must give him credit that he managed to withstand the pressure and lingered on the edge of the abyss rather than falling in headfirst. And, although in 1996 he returned anew to the Atlanticist model and entered into the Khasavyurt Accord with the separatists, cancelling with the stroke of a pen all the previous military successes of the federal forces, by the end of the 1990s he had demonstrated again that he could not be included unreservedly in the category of Russia's destroyers. He appointed as his successor Vladimir Putin, who, beginning in 2000, would implement a completely different geopolitical policy. After turning power over to Putin, Yeltsin entrusted to him the fate of his own place in Russia's history as well. And it may be that this became his geopolitical testament.

We will consider the significance of this testament in the next chapter.

CHAPTER IV

The Geopolitics of the 2000s: The Phenomenon of Putin

The Structure of the Poles of Force in Chechnya in 1996–1999

After the Khasavyurt Accord, Chechen separatists had an opportunity to rebuild their power structures and consolidate their power over the entire territory of the Chechen Republic. Gradually, three competing tendencies arose among them:

1. Moderate circles of a national-democratic orientation, given priority support by the West and attempting to play by Western rules (A. Maskhadov, A. Zakayev, and others);

2. Representatives of national-traditionalist Islam, oriented toward *teips*[135] and *wirds*[136] (A. Kadyrov, K. A. Noukhayev, and others);

3. Radical Wahhabis,[137] who considered themselves a part of the global network of Islamic fundamentalism, fighting for the establishment of

---

135 A *teip* refers to a clan in the Chechen and Ingush regions.—Ed.

136 A *wird*, in Sufism (mystical Islam) is a subdivision of a *tariqa*, or a school or order of Sufism.—Ed.

137 Wahhabism is an extremely strict, literal interpretation of Sunni Islam. Many militant jihadis around the world claim to follow its teachings, or an ideology derived from it.—Ed.

a global Islamic state (S. Basayev, M. Udugov, the "Black Khattab," and others).

Geopolitically, all three forces were oriented in various directions: the national-democrats, to Atlanticism; the traditionalists, to the local population and its foundations; the Wahhabis, to the global network of radical fundamentalists.

The Geopolitics of Islam

Radical Islam experienced a rebirth in the 1970s, when American and British intelligence agencies started to use it to oppose socialist and pro-Soviet tendencies in the Islamic world and, in particular, in Afghanistan. Thus, Zbigniew Brzezinski began training the Islamic radicals and, in particular, the representatives of Al-Qaeda in the military training camps of the anti-Soviet *mujahideen*. Up to a point, Islamic fundamentalism thus fulfilled the function of a regional *instrument in the hands of the Atlanticists.*

Geopolitically, the Islamic world itself belongs mostly to the coastal zone (Rimland), which makes it a zone of the opposition of two powers: the Land and the Sea. In this "coastal zone," two contrary orientations meet: orientation toward the West and orientation toward the East. During the "Cold War," the representatives of liberal Islam and the radical fundamentalists (in particular, the Wahhabis and Salafists,[138] who prevailed in Saudi Arabia, a reliable regional partner of the USA in the Middle East) were sea-directed. The regimes oriented toward socialism and the USSR, such as the countries of Islamic socialism or the "Ba'athists" (the Pan-Arab Party, which stands for the unification of all Arab governments into a unified political formation) were land-directed. After the Shi'ite revolution of 1979, Iran became a special case, when the radical Shi'ites, led by the Ayatollah Khomeini, took the place of the pro-American Shah. Iran's position was strictly "coastal": the Iranian slogan "neither East nor West, only the Islamic Republic"

---

138 Salafism is a fundamentalist interpretation of Sunni theology.—Ed.

meant a rejection of closer relations with both the capitalist West and the socialist East.

But after the collapse of the USSR and the global, pro-Soviet geopolitical network, radical Islam forfeited its main geopolitical function to the Atlanticists. Meanwhile, it gathered momentum, and its American and British curators were unable to reduce it to nothing. Ties with Atlanticism were often preserved; however, the Wahabbi-Salafist circles gradually gained autonomy and became an influential and independent force. Since the main enemy, the USSR, no longer existed, Islamic fundamentalists began to gradually carry out local attacks on their former patrons, the USA. In the case of Chechnya, Wahhabism, spread there from the end of the 1980s until the end of the 1990s as an independent and influential force, fulfilled a classic function by serving the interests of the civilization of the Sea in its aspiration to weaken the civilization of Land as much as possible and to dismember Russia. That is why the alliance of the national democrats of Maskhadov[139] with the Wahhabi circles ultimately shared a common geopolitical denominator: both objectively played into the hands of the Atlanticists.

The Bombing of Homes in Moscow, the Incursion into Dagestan, and Putin's Coming to Power

The Wahhabi pole started to form in Chechnya at the end of the 1980s, and from the beginning it was not limited to the territory of Chechnya. Moreover, the center of the spread of Wahhabism was initially neighboring Dagestan. One of the representatives of the first Dagestani Wahhabis was Bagaudin Kebedov, who had already established close contacts with the

---

139 Aslan Maskhadov (1951–2005) was a leader and military commander of the Chechen independence movement and was the third President of the Chechen Republic of Ichkeria.—Ed.

mercenary Arab Salafist, Khattab[140] (who later proved to have close ties to the CIA) and the Chechen Field Commanders during the First Chechen War. In Grozny in April 1998, with the participation of Kebedov and his supporters, a constitutional convention of the "Congress of the *Narodi* of Ichkeria and Dagestan" (CNID) was held, the leader of which was Shamil Basayev. Its main task was "the liberation of the Muslim Caucasus from the imperialist Russian yoke" (an altogether Atlanticist thesis). Under the aegis of the CNID, paramilitary units were created, including the "Islamic International Peacekeeping Brigade," which Khattab commanded. Wahhabis began to create an armed underground in Dagestan, and by 1999 their influence became critically high. In 1999, Kebedov's fighters began to penetrate Dagestan in small groups and established military bases and arms depots in hard-to-reach, mountainous hamlets. After his travels to Dagestan, the Prime Minister of the Russian Federation, S. Stepashin, was so impressed by the influence of the Wahhabis that he desperately exclaimed, "Russia, it seems, has lost Dagestan."

On August 7, 1999, subdivisions of the "Islamic International Peacekeeping Brigade" of Basayev and Khattab, 400–500 fighters, entered the Botlikhsky region of Dagestan without difficulty and seized a group of villages (Ansalta, Rakhata, Tando, Shodroda, and Godoberi) after announcing the beginning of the operation "Imam Ghazi Mohammed." With difficulty, federal troops and local armed militias were able to recapture a few towns by the end of August. In response, early September 1999 (4–16), these Wahhabi circles blew up a series of residential complexes in Moscow, Buynaksk and Volgodonsk. These terrorist attacks were planned and carried out by the representatives of the illegal paramilitary "Islamic Institute of the Caucusus," Shamil Basayev, Emir al-Khattab, and Abu Umarov. 307 people died and more than 1,700 people were injured in these attacks.

---

140 Ibn al-Khattab (1969–2002) was a Saudi-born jihadi who fought against the Russians in Afghanistan during the 1980s, and later received training in Al Qaeda camps there. He went to Chechnya in 1995 and fought against the Russians in both wars, and also in the Dagestan War. He was assassinated by the FSB in March 2002.—Ed.

On September 5, 1999, contingents of Chechen fighters under the command of Basayev and Khattab again entered Dagestan. These operations were given the name "Imam Gamzat-Bek."

This was the decisive, critical moment in recent Russian history. Separatist Chechnya, which had received breathing space after the Khasavyurt Accord, became the source for the spread of an active separatism under the Wahhabi banner all over the Northern Caucasus, especially in Dagestan. Things were aggravated by the uncertainty and wavering of the federal center, at the head of which stood the hopelessly ill Boris Yeltsin, who now barely understood the world around him, immersed in an environment of pro-Western agents of influence blocking any sovereign initiative. This vacillation allowed the militants to carry out daring attacks and to conduct terrorism far beyond the borders of Chechnya, invading the territory of Dagestan and bombing houses in Russian cities, Moscow in particular. This was the critical line which could have signified the start of Russia's headlong collapse. Russia seemed to be about to disappear as a *geopolitical whole*. If the daring acts of the Wahhabis were successful, other Islamic regions, and behind them, many other territories in the Russian Federation, would promptly follow the example of the North Caucasian republics.

In this period, Yeltsin began to recognize the gravity of his situation and that of the corrupt, oligarchic, and pro-Western elite that surrounded him ("the Seven"). He looked feverishly for a successor, but understood in time that Sergei Stepashin, appointed Prime Minister of Russia from May until August 1999, was not capable of coping with things. At that moment he chose in favor of the then little-known bureaucrat, the former Deputy to the Mayor of Saint Petersburg Anatoly Sobchak, Vladimir Vladimirovich Putin, the leader of the Federal Security Service (FSB). In August 1999, Yeltsin, unexpectedly for many, appointed Putin as Acting Prime Minister and as his successor to the post of President of the Russian Federation. This choice cardinally changed Russia's fate and became the point at which a sharp change was made in its geopolitical course. Putin came to power when seemingly nothing could stop Russia's fall into the abyss.

Once he assumed office, Putin turned his primary attention immediately to Chechnya and the war blazing in Dagestan. Thus began the Second Chechen War.

The Second Chechen War

The invasion of Dagestan and the attacks on residential complexes occurred during the first days of Putin's administration. Things became critical, and Putin had to make a fundamental gesture: either to accept the tendencies gathering strength as proper and inevitable, or to attempt to change matters and turn back the course of events. This moment had a colossal geopolitical significance for the whole history of Russia.

Putin chose in favor of restoring Russia's territorial integrity and took this path firmly and without wavering (in complete contrast with Yeltsin's manner of rule).

In the middle of September, Putin decided to conduct a military operation to destroy the Chechen militants. On September 18, Chechnya's borders were blockaded by Russian troops. On September 23, at Putin's bidding, Russia's President, now Boris Yeltsin, signed a decree "On Measures to Improve the Efficiency of Counter-Terrorism Operations in the North Caucasus Region of the Russian Federation," which created military units in the North Caucasus to carry out counter-terrorism operations. On September 23, Russian troops began a large-scale bombardment of Grozny and its outskirts, and on September 30 they entered the territory of Chechnya. Thus began the Second Chechen War.

In this campaign the Kremlin based itself on two principles. The first was the radical destruction of all separatist paramilitaries and the suppression of all hotbeds of resistance, with the goal of establishing control over the territory of Chechnya and returning it to the Russian administrative zone. The second was "the Chechenization of the conflict": to win over the forces minimally connected to the foreign Atlanticist centers of control to its own side (in 2000, the former supporter of the separatists, the Chief Mufti of Chechnya, the traditionalist Akhmad Kadyrov, became the head of the administration of Chechnya, and was loyal to Russia). The radical separatists responded to this strategy by appealing for help from foreign mercenaries and the West. Indirectly, this undermined their position among the majority of the Chechen population, strangers to the imported Wahhabi ideology and to liberal-democratic Western values.

We see that Putin's policy in the Second Chechen War had a clearly Eurasian, land-based geopolitical character and logically opposed the forces striving to weaken centripetal tendencies and to dismember Russia. From now on, this was the main vector of Putin's policy. This sharply differed from Yeltsin's course and was at the basis of the fast-growing popularity of the new Russian leader. We see this in Moscow's unyielding will to return Chechnya to Russian control (on September 27, Putin categorically rejected the possibility of a meeting between himself and the leader of the Chechen Republic of Ichkeria, explaining that, "There will be no meetings to allow the militants to lick their wounds"). We also see it in the absence of influence of Western agents on the situation (to whom Putin would not listen), in Putin's taking account of geopolitical factors, in the readiness to oppose the West's pressure, and in the skillful employment of various political, ideological, and geopolitical tendencies in the internal centers of influence and authority.

All these factors together led to the total success of this strategy. Russian troops entered Chechnya both from the North and from the side of Ingushetia, and gradually liberated one population center after another from the militants. The brothers, Field Commander Yamadayev and the Mufti of Chechnya, Akhmad Kadyrov, surrendered the vital strategic center of Gudermes on November 11 without a fight.

On December 26, the battle for Grozny began, ending in the capture of the city only in February 2000. After this the gradual liberation of the entire remaining territory of Chechnya from the separatists followed; first the flatlands, then the mountainous regions. On February 29, 2000 the first Deputy Commander of the united group of federal forces, Colonel General Gennady Troshev, announced the end of full-scale military operations in Chechnya, although this was probably a symbolic gesture: battles continued in many regions of Chechnya for a long time thereafter.

On March 20, on the eve of the presidential elections, Vladimir Putin visited Chechnya, at that time under the control of the federal forces. And on April 20, the First Deputy Commander of the General Staff, Colonel General Valery Manilov, announced the end of the military element of the counter-terrorism operation in Chechnya and the shift to special operations.

In Grozny on May 9, at the "Dynamo" stadium, where a parade was taking place in honor of Victory Day,[141] a powerful explosion took place, killing the President of Chechnya, Akhmad Kadyrov. Afterwards, the separatists continued to carry out sporadic attacks around Chechnya and beyond its borders.

On March 8, 2005, during an FSB special operation in Tolstoy-Yurt, the unrecognized "President" of the Chechen Republic of Ichkeria, Aslan Maskhadov, was annihilated, and on June 10, 2006, one of the terrorist leaders, Shamil Basayev, was killed.

In 2007 the son of Akhmad Kadyrov, Ramzan Kadyrov, became the leader of Chechnya at age 30, carrying on his father's policies.

The geopolitical results of the Second Chechen War were the shutdown of the extreme form of separatist trends in the North Caucasus, the preservation of Russia's territorial integrity, the destruction of the Chechen separatists' major bases of power, and the establishment of the federal government's control over the entire territory of the Russian Federation.

---

141 May 9 is the date that Russia and the other former Soviet republics celebrate their victory over Germany in the Second World War, when Germany's unconditional surrender to the Soviet Union went into effect.—Ed.

In practice, this was the turning point of Russia's post-Soviet history. From the end of the 1980s until the start of the Second Chechen War and the appointment of Vladimir Putin, Russia was steadily *losing* its geopolitical positions, ceding one geopolitical position after another, until it nearly led to the fall of the Russian Federation itself. The First Chechen War put the brakes on this process, but did not make it irreversible. The conclusion of the Khasavyurt Accord rendered all previous efforts null and again made the death of Russia as a government a real prospect. Basayev and Khattab's attacks on Dagestan and the attacks on homes in Buynaksk, Moscow, and Volgodonsk meant the imminent and inevitable collapse of the government. In such a situation, the new political leader, Putin, took a firm position, directed toward stopping this destructive chain of geopolitical catastrophes, managing to overcome the deepest crisis, reestablish lost positions, and thereby open a new page in Russia's geopolitical history.

The Geopolitical Significance of Putin's Reforms

Other steps taken by Putin during his first two terms as President between 2000 and 2004 were generally marked by the same sovereign, Eurasian spirit. This approach, clearly followed in the Second Chechen War, was developed and consolidated in a series of reforms that changed the political, ideological, and geopolitical course along which the country had been moving under Gorbachev and Yeltsin. The main symbolic acts in Putin's reforms, endowed with clear geopolitical content, were the following:

1. Censure of the policy taken in the 1990s toward the de-sovereignization of Russia and the virtual introduction of foreign rule, with a corresponding proclamation of sovereignty as contemporary Russia's highest value;

2. The strengthening of the shaken territorial unity of the Russian Federation through a series of measures, including firm military actions against the Chechen separatists, the consolidation of Moscow's

position in the North Caucasus on the whole, and the introduction of seven Federal Districts with the goal of excluding separatist attempts anywhere in Russia; the elimination of the concept of "sovereignty" in the legislative acts of subjects of the Federation and national republics, and the transition to a system of appointing the heads of the Federation's subjects instead of the old model of electing them (this measure was introduced after the tragic events in Beslan, when middle school children became hostages of the terrorists).

3. The banishment of the most odious oligarchs, who had been virtually all-powerful in the 1990s, out of the country (B. Berezovsky, V. Gusinsky, L. Nevzlin) and the criminal persecution of others for the crimes they committed (M. Khodorkovsky, P. Lebedev, etc.); the nationalization of several large raw-materials monopolies, while compelling the oligarchs to play the game according to the government's rules by recognizing the legitimacy of the policy of strengthening Russia's sovereignty;

4. A frank and often impartial dialogue with the USA and the West, with a condemnation of double standards, American hegemony and the unipolar world, contrasted with an orientation toward multipolarity and a cooperation with all forces (in particular, with continental Europe) interested in opposing American hegemony;

5. A change in the information policy of the major national media, which used to broadcast the views of their oligarchic owners, but were now called on to take government interests into account;

6. A reconsideration of the nihilistic attitude toward Russian history that then prevailed, based on the uncritical acceptance of the Western liberal-democratic approach, through inculcating respect for and deference toward Russian history's most significant landmarks and figures (in particular, the establishment of the new holiday, November 4, The Day of National Unity, in honor of the liberation of Moscow from Polish-Lithuanian occupation by the Second People's Militia);

7. Support for the processes of integration in the post-Soviet space and the commencement of Russia's operations in the countries of the CIS; also the formation or resuscitation of integrating structures, such as the "Eurasian Economic Community," the "Collective Security Treaty Organization," the "Common Economic Space," etc.;

8. The normalization of party life by prohibiting oligarchic structures from political lobbying on behalf of their private and corporate interests using the parliamentary parties;

9. The elaboration of a consolidated government policy in the sphere of energy resources, which transformed Russia into a mighty energy state capable of influencing economic processes in the neighboring regions of Europe and Asia; plans for laying gas and oil pipelines to the West and the East became a visible expression of the energy geopolitics of the new Russia, repeating the main force-lines of classical geopolitics on a new level.

These reforms elicited stiff resistance from the forces oriented toward the West and the civilization of the Sea in the era of Yeltsin and Gorbachev which comprised, either consciously or unconsciously, *a network of agents of influence of thalassocracy,* carriers of the liberal-democratic worldview and global-capitalist tendencies. This resistance to Putin's course was manifest in opposition from the Right-wing parties (Yabloko, Pravoe Delo); in the appearance of a new, radical opposition of the ultraliberal and openly pro-American kind, sponsored by the USA and Western funds ("Dissenters"); in the intense anti-Russian actions of the oligarchs who had been removed from power; in pressure from the USA and the West on the Kremlin to prevent the development of this trend; in the active resistance to the strategy of the Russian Federation in the CIS on the side of pro-Western, pro-American forces, such as the "Orange Revolution" in Ukraine, the "Rose Revolution" in Tbilisi, Moldova's anti-Russian policy, and so forth.

Putin and his policy expressed the geopolitical, sociological, and ideo-logical tendencies corresponding, mostly, to the main features of the *civi-lization of Land and to the constants of Russian geopolitical history*. If the actions of Gorbachev and Yeltsin were in glaring *conflict* with the trajectory of Russian geopolitics, then Putin's rule, on the contrary, restored Russia's traditional path, returning it to its customary continental, tellurocratic or-bit. Thus, with Putin, the Heartland got a new historic opportunity, and the process of establishing a unipolar world hit a real obstacle. It became clear that despite all the weakness and confusion, Russia-Eurasia did not ultimately disappear from the geopolitical map of the world and is still, though in a reduced condition, *the core of an alternative civilization,* the civilization of Land.

September 11th: Geopolitical Consequences and Putin's Response

If Putin took on a tellurocratic spirit, which became the most noteworthy feature of his rule, then in the details he often departed from this policy.

The first such deviation became apparent after the tragic events of September 11, 2001, when New York and Washington were subjected to unprecedented attacks by Islamic radicals (as the commission that studied the rationale and perpetrators of the attack concluded). Putin decided to support the USA and rendered diplomatic and political aid for the ensuing invasion and occupation of Afghanistan by American forces. The forces of the Northern Alliance, then fighting the Taliban, were in close contact with the Russian intelligence services, and when NATO invaded Afghanistan, Russia acted as a liaison with the occupying forces, which became one of the factors contributing to the rapid overthrow of the Taliban.

Putin probably calculated that the radical Islam of the Afghan Taliban was a substantial threat to Russia and the countries of Central Asia in the Russian zone of influence, and that an American invasion in such a situation would be a blow against those forces that had caused Russia such unpleas-antness. Moreover, in his support for Bush, who had announced a "crusade" against international terrorism, Putin strove to undermine the system of political, diplomatic, informational, and economic support that had been coming to the separatists of Chechnya and the North Caucasus from the West; previously, in supporting the Chechen militants, the Americans had been aiding those forces that had brought their own country so painful a blow. Thus, closer relations with the USA and, correspondingly, with the Atlanticist pole had a practical character for Putin, and he did not abrogate his fundamental orientation toward tellurocracy. However, one cannot but notice a serious contradiction in such a tactic: approving the American occupation of Afghanistan, Russia was left with, instead of only one hostile force (the radical Islamists) on the southern frontiers of its strategic zone of influence, also another, more serious one in the form of US military bases. This was the direct presence in Russia's areas of influence of its primary strategic opponents on the geopolitical map of the world. If Russia strove to build an alternative multipolar system against the unipolar world, it should never have allowed the deployment of a US military contingent in immediate proximity to its southern borders and to the borders of the countries of Central Asia that are allied with Russia.

The Paris-Berlin-Moscow Axis

After receiving support from Russia, the USA next invaded and occupied Iraq as well, for no reason whatsoever, which evoked a natural protest from Russia, France, and Germany. This anti-American coalition received the name "the Paris-Berlin-Moscow axis," and in a short time it seemed that the creation of a *European-Eurasian multipolar bloc* was occurring, aimed at the containment of unipolar American hegemony. This prospect worried the Americans a great deal, so they promptly undertook a series of efforts directed at tearing this coalition down as quickly as possible. The Paris-Berlin-Moscow Axis represented an *outline of a tellurocratic alliance,* recalling the earlier Eurasian projects of the European geopolitical continentalists such as Jean Thiriart, with his "Euro-Soviet Empire from Vladivostok to Dublin," or Alain de Benoist, who had called for an alliance of continental Europe with Russia.

Anyhow, the invasion of Iraq showed that the USA acts only in its own interests and was not planning to take Russia into consideration, despite Russia's concessions in Afghanistan. Moreover, Washington never ended its support for the Chechen and Caucasian separatists, and Zbigniew Brzezinski explained rather cynically that only those who fight with the USA should be reckoned among "international terrorists," while those who weaken the competitors and adversaries of the USA (in particular, the fundamentalists of the North Caucasus) must be excluded from this category and equated with "freedom fighters."

If we assess the balance of Putin's demarche according to his closer relations with the USA, we can say that overall it produced ambiguous results and was most likely a geopolitical error. Russia won almost nothing from this, but lost the clarity and consistency of its tellurocratic policy, which had been emphasized so clearly and sharply by the first acts of Putin's reforms immediately after his coming to power. Against the general background of the tellurocratic strategy, this was neither a justifiable nor effective retreat from that policy. It is telling that the representatives of Eurasian Russian geopolitics then cautioned Putin against his policy toward the USA,[142] predicting the course of events that indeed took place a short time later. Thus, in the context of Putin's tellurocratic geopolitics, elements that reject its logic appear, suggesting that even after Putin came to power, the network of Atlanticist agents was preserved in Russia. Despite having lost its leading position and undivided influence over the highest political authorities as was the case in the era of Gorbachev and Yeltsin, it yet retains significant positions and resources. After September 11, many Russian experts actively supported Putin and his decisions, and that same group of experts strongly condemned his initiative to create a "Paris-Berlin-Moscow" axis during

---

142 *The Geopolitics of Terror: A Collection of Materials by the Eurasian Movement Devoted to Analyzing the Terrorist Attacks in New York on September 11, 2001* (Moscow, 2002).

the American-British invasion of Iraq. The fact that such experts retained their influence in Russia and received an open platform for the expression of their positions in the federal media confirmed this suspicion. Despite the abrupt change of course from a thalassocratic one, leading to a quick death, to a tellurocratic one oriented toward the rebirth of the civilization of Land and the position of the Heartland, it became clear after the events of September 11, 2001, and Moscow's response to them, that amidst these radical geopolitical reforms, the fight for influence over the Russian government had not ended, and Putin's reforms could deviate from the projected path.

The Atlanticist Network of Influence in Putin's Russia

The abrupt change of course of Russian policy during Putin's rule, following a vector that was the opposite of the one that had preceded it, was nevertheless not fixed, neither in Russia's strategic doctrine, nor in the government's ideological programs and manifestos, nor in the specification of national interests and the methods of their realization, nor in the systematic increase in Russia's geopolitical, economic, and political might. Putin normalized the situation and ended the most destructive and catastrophic phenomena. This was the meaning of his mission. But there was no real project for Russia's future geopolitical development, and no Eurasian agreement was worked out during the two terms of his presidency. Everything was limited by practical steps, directed toward controlling the most destructive processes without an orderly and consistent civilizational plan. Putin adapted himself to the situation, striving at every opportunity to strengthen Russia's position, but if no such situations turned up, he focused his attention on the resolution of purely technical problems.

Thus the specific *practical-technical style* of his administration was worked out. The general line of development of his policy was directed *along a Eurasian, land-based, tellurocratic vector*, and this predetermined the primary substance of his reforms. But this line did not receive a conceptual and theoretical formulation. Instead, the policy was carried out entirely by technical political methods; often one thing was proclaimed, while in practice something entirely different was done. Official discourse contained deliberate or accidental contradictions and appeals to a thalassocratic system of values; liberalism and Westernism were alternated with patriotism, tellurocracy, and the affirmation of the values and uniqueness of Russian civilization. Overall, this produced an eclectic atmosphere, and all sharp corners were avoided by means of confusing public relations campaigns. It is common to tie this style of contradiction, of purely technical and vacuous policy, to the Kremlin's main ideologue during Putin's reign, Vladislav Surkov.[143] Surkov took strict care that in almost every political declaration, appeals to incompatible values and sociological, political, and geopolitical models were preserved. There were appeals to statehood and liberalism, to the West and to Russian uniqueness, to hierarchical authority and to democratization, to sovereignty and to globalization, to a multipolar world and to a unipolar one, to Atlanticism and to Eurasianism. All the while, none of these orientations was supposed to have any greater validity than its opposite.

The pool of experts at the Kremlin was preserved unchanged from the 1990s and represented the prevalence of liberal and pro-Western, pro-American analysts, and were often also the West's direct agents of influence. It is revealing that, from the end of 2002, the journal *Russia in Global Affairs* started to circulate, openly declaring that it was a subsidiary publication of the American journal *Foreign Affairs*, published by the Council on Foreign Relations, the center for the elaboration of the Atlanticist, thalassocratic, and globalist strategy. During Putin's presidency, this journal was not only published officially and openly, detailing the main geopolitical and strategic projects of the USA for the unipolar organization of the

---

143 Vladislav Surkov (b. 1964) was First Deputy of the Presidential Administration from 1999 until 2011, and is regarded as the chief ideologue and architect of the Russian political system as it exists today.—Ed.

world, it also included on its editorial committee the following exceedingly influential and high-placed figures: A. L. Adamishin, the extraordinary and plenipotentiary ambassador of the Russian Federation; A. G.
Arbatov, the Director of the Center of International Security of IMEMO;
A. G. Vishnevsky, the Director of the Center for Demography and Human
Ecology of the Institute of Economic Forecasting; A. D. Zhukova, First
Deputy Chairperson of the Russian Federation; S. B. Ivanov, once secretary
of the Security Council of the Russian Federation, later Minister of Defense
and First Deputy Prime Minister; S. A. Karaganov, who was curator of the
publication and Chairman of the Presidium of the Council on Foreign and
Defense Policy (created as an affiliate of the CFR in Russia in 1991); A. A.
Kokoshin, a distinguished figure of "United Russia"; Y. I. Kuz'minov, chancellor of the State University Higher School of Economics; S. V. Lavrov,
Foreign Minister of the Russian Federation, an excellent and plenipotentiary ambassador of the Russian Federation; V. P. Lukin, Commission of
the Russian Federation for Human Rights; F. A. Luk'yanova, the editor-in-
chief of the journal *Russia in Global Affairs*; V. A. May, the chancellor of the
Academy of the *Narodni* Economy under the Government of the Russian
Federation; V. A. Nikonov, the President of the "Policy" and "Russian
World" foundations; V. V. Posner, the President of the Academy of Russian
Television; S. E. Prikhod'ko, assistant to the President of the Russian
Federation; V. A. Ryzhkov, former Deputy and eminent member of the liberal opposition; A. V. Torkunov, chancellor of the Moscow State Institute
of International Relations; I. M. Khakamada, a politician of the ultra-liberal opposition; and I. J. Jurgens, Director of the Institute of Contemporary
Development, as well as Vice-President and Executive Secretary of the
Russian Union of Industrialists and Entrepreneurs (Employers) and others.

It is difficult to imagine that such highly placed actors — among whom
we also see the President's counsellor on foreign policy, the Minister of
Foreign Affairs, highly placed officials of the special services, and elite
managers from the scientific community — did not know the nature of

the editorial board of the organ they had chosen to join. Consequently, this group, which united those closest to Putin with ardent members of the opposition, was consciously formed on a pro-American, thalassocratic, liberal, globalist, and Atlanticist basis. After this, it is not surprising that Putin's Eurasian and tellurocratic policy did not receive a fitting and consistent formulation: the American network of agents of influence, which reached to the heights of Russia's authorities, immediately extinguished any attempt to develop Putin's actions to the level of a system or to fix its logic as a program, project, doctrine, or strategy.

And again, the manager responsible for domestic policy in the President's administration, Vladislav Surkov, played the key role in ensuring that no serious steps toward the creation of such a strategy took place, and were instead replaced by empty tricks of political manipulation. Being very experienced in such techniques and understanding how information and image strategies work, he single-handedly established a political system in Russia in which everything was knowingly based on postmodern paradoxes, on the conscious entanglement of all political forces, and on hybrid crosses of patriotic elements with liberal-Western ones.

We can raise the question: were Surkov and the highly placed Russian bureaucrats of the first tier acting independently when they supported Atlanticism and the consistent sabotage of the development of a real strategy? Instead, there were only caricatures and vapid public relations events in the spirit of Strategy 2020[144] or the pompous and pointless forums held under the aegis of "United Russia."[145] Or did Putin consciously veil his reforms behind the smokescreen of an endless sequence of pointless and contradictory pronouncements and actions, confusing both his enemies and his friends? We cannot answer this question today, since time must pass for many things to become clear. We cannot rule out that this was his policy for the disinformation of the adversary (Atlanticism, the USA, globalism)

---

144 A long-term plan for Russia's economic development.—Ed.

145 United Russia is currently the largest political party in Russia, and is the party of Putin.—Ed.

and had been intended to divert attention while he latently undertook a series of concrete steps directed toward securing Russia's might, accumulating its resources, and consolidating its energy management and major economic policies. But we are probably dealing with a case of the planned sabotage of Putin's Eurasian initiatives by Atlanticism's agents of influence, retained at the upper levels of power and at the head of the highest institutions of learning from the time of Gorbachev and Yeltsin, when orientation toward the West and to the unipolar world was the official policy of the Russian government.

The fact that Putin's strategy did not receive its proper formulation, while the influence of the pro-American, liberal, thalassocratic networks were not ended and were preserved in full measure during Putin's rule, should be stated as an empirical fact and an important circumstance in the general geopolitical evaluation of his governance.

Besides the editorial committee of the journal *Russia in Global Affairs,* the most influential experts of an openly Atlanticist persuasion (in part overlapping the membership of its editorial committee) made up the basis of the intellectual club "Valdai,"[146] with whom Putin, and later his successor, Medvedev, regularly met. The peculiarity of this group is that American and European experts were included side by side with Russian agents of influence, including a group of figures who had a direct and manifest relation to American intelligence agencies; in particular, A. Cohen,[147] A. Kuchins,[148] C. Kupchan,[149] and F. Hill.[150]

---

146 The Valdai International Discussion Club was founded in 2004 to provide a forum for international experts to gather and discuss the future of Russia.—Ed.

147 A senior researcher at the American "Heritage Foundation," specializing in the study of Russia, Eurasia, and international energy security.

148 Director of the Russian-Eurasian program and a senior researcher at the Carnegie Foundation for International Peace USA.

149 Director of the Europe and Eurasia section of the "Eurasia Group."

150 Heads the "Russian section" of the National Intelligence Council.

The Post-Soviet Space: Integration

In the period of Putin's rule, the geopolitical situation of the post-Soviet space intensified. Here we see two opposed tendencies.

On one hand, with Putin's coming to power, the processes of integrating the group of CIS countries with Russia's center began on different levels simultaneously:

• economically: the creation of a Eurasian Economic Community (Russia, Kazakhstan, Belarus, Tadzhikistan, and Kirghizia), the "Common Economic Space" (Russia, Belarus, Kazakhstan, with Ukraine being invited), and Customs Union (Russia, Kazakhstan, Belarus);

• militarily and strategically: the "Social Contract on Collective Security" (Russia, Kazakhstan, Belarus, Tadzhikistan, Kirghizia, and Armenia).

Moreover, we should mention the more avant-garde project of political integration along the model of the European Union, advanced by the President of Kazakhstan, Nursultan Nazarbayev,[151] already in 1994, but completely rejected by the pro-Western Russian elite at that time. This project received the name of the "Eurasian Union." This project was not openly supported by Putin until the fall of 2011, but the idea of closer relations between the countries of the post-Soviet space was not rejected by Putin even before then. If the post-Soviet space in previous stages (the former USSR, and before that of the Russian Empire) was transformed in only one area — namely, toward a weakening and destruction of those forces that united these parts of a formerly single whole — then after Putin's coming to power, the opposite initiatives were also clearly emphasized: integration, closer relations, the strengthening of coordination, and so on.

---

151 Nursultan Nazarbayev (b. 1940) has been the President of Kazakhstan since 1989.—Ed.

There were two more organizations of an integrational kind: the Union State of Russia and Belarus[152] and the Shanghai Cooperation Organization (SCO),[153] into which China and the countries of the Eurasian Economic Community entered, beside Russia. From the beginning, Putin's relations with Belarus and its President, A. G. Lukashenko, did not come together, and therefore this integrational initiative did not develop in the proper way, remaining in that nominal condition in which it was announced in Yeltsin's time. This can be regarded as another sign of the inconsistency of Putin's implementation of the Eurasian policy, for which the alliance with Belarus and the prospective political unification with it would be a logical and necessary step (Russia would receive access to Western territories, strategically necessary for the conduct of its European policy, which Russian leaders at all stages of our geopolitical history understood perfectly well, from Ivan III[154] to Stalin).

As concerns the SCO, Putin, on the contrary, undertook a series of steps toward an intensification of a strategic partnership with China in regional questions, including a series of small-scale, but symbolically significant military exercises. The alliance with China was built wholly on multipolar logic and was unambiguously oriented to indicating a possible way to create strategic opposition to the unipolar world and American hegemony.

The Geopolitics of the Color Revolutions

In the same period, opposite geopolitical tendencies, "color revolutions," began to unfold intensely. Their meaning consisted in bringing to power openly anti-Russian, pro-Western, and often nationalistic political forces in

---

152 The Union State is a commonwealth that was formed between Russia and Belarus in 1996. While Russia has attempted to strengthen the Union, Belarus has remained resistant, fearing for its independence. Discussion of the Union State has been subsumed into Russia's larger project of a Eurasian Union for the region.—Ed.

153 The SCO was formed in 2001 as a military and economic alliance between China, Russia, Kazakhstan, Kyrgyzstan, Tajikistan, and Uzbekistan.—Ed.

154 Ivan III (1440–1505) ended Mongol rule over Russia and tripled the size of Russia's territory. He was called "the gatherer of the Russian lands."—Ed.

the countries of the CIS, and thereby finally tearing these countries away from Russia, to frustrate integration, and in the long term to include them in NATO as occurred in the Baltic countries. The peculiarity of these revolutions was that they were all aimed at bringing about closer relations of the countries in which they occurred with the USA and the West, and they followed the method of "non-violent resistance,"[155] which American strategists had elaborated in the framework of the "Freedom House" project.[156] This was carried out through subversive measures and the organization of revolutions that had been executed in the Third World under the direction of the CIA.

In November 2003, the "Rose Revolution" happened in Georgia, where the evasive Eduard Shevardnadze, who had been wavering between the West and Moscow, was replaced by the strictly pro-Western, radically Atlanticist, and pro-American politician Mikhail Saakashvili. An active role in the events of the "Rose Revolution" was played by the youth organization Kmara (literally "Enough!"), which acted in accordance with the ideas of the primary theoretician of analogous networks of protest organizations, Gene Sharp, and with the methods of "Freedom House." These techniques had already been tested in other places; in particular in Yugoslavia during the overthrow of Slobodan Milošević, using the pro-Western Serbian youth organization Otpor.

After coming to power, Saakashvili headed immediately for a swift deviation from Russia and for closer relations with the USA and NATO. He set about actively sabotaging any initiatives for integrating into the framework of the CIS and attempted to revive the essentially anti-Russian unification of the governments of the CIS with the GUAM bloc: Georgia,

---

155 Gene Sharp, *From Dictatorship to Democracy: The Strategy and Tactics of Liberation* (Boston: Albert Einstein Institution, 1994).

156 Freedom House is an American non-governmental organization that was founded in 1941. Its stated goal is to spread democratic ideals throughout the world. It receives funding from the US government, and many countries have accused it of interfering with their internal affairs, claiming that Freedom House has links to the State Department and the CIA.

Ukraine, Azerbaijan, and Moldova. Saakashvili's circle consisted mainly of advisors who had received their education abroad and were not historically connected to the Soviet experience. After this time, Georgia stood in the avant-garde of the Atlanticist strategy in the post-Soviet space and took an active role in the opposition to Eurasianist tendencies. Putin and his policy became Georgia's main adversaries. Later, this spilled over into the events of August 2008, when it became the Russia-Georgian War.

In December 2004, in a similar scenario, the "Orange Revolution" happened in Ukraine. Elections were held, in a race between the protégé of Kuchma,[157] who followed an ambivalent policy between the West and Russia; V. Yanukovich;[158] and the entirely pro-Western and strictly anti-Russian nationalist politicians, V. Yushchenko[159] and Y. Timoshenko.[160] The forces were approximately even, and the outcome was decided by the mobilization of the masses and particularly by those youths who supported the "orange" cause through massive demonstrations, organized along Gene Sharp's model. The youth movement Pora[161] played an important role in these processes. After Yushchenko's victory, Ukraine took a firm anti-Russian position, started to actively counteract any Russian initiatives, began an attack on the use of the Russian language, and began to rewrite history, representing Ukrainians as a "people colonized by Russians." Geopolitically,

---

157 Leonid Kuchma (b. 1938) was President of Ukraine from 1994 until 2005. He sought a balanced approach to Ukrainian foreign relations that would include relations with both the EU and the CIS.—Ed.

158 Viktor Yanukovich (b. 1950) initially won the 2004 election, but widespread allegations of election fraud led to the Orange Revolution, and Yuschchenko became President instead. He was elected in 2010, but was overthrown by the Euromaidan revolution in February 2014 following his announcement of his plan to abandon integration with the EU in favor of closer economic relations with the CIS.—Ed.

159 Viktor Yuschchenko (b. 1954) was President of Ukraine from 2005 until 2010. Following an assassination attempt which nearly killed him, he was brought to power following the Orange Revolution.—Ed.

160 Yulia Timoshenko (b. 1960) was one of the leaders of the Orange Revolution and served twice as Prime Minister of Ukraine, subsequently.—Ed.

161 A. Alexandrov, M. Murashkin, S. Kara-Murza, and S. Telegin, *The Export of Revolution: Saakashvili, Yushchenko* (Moscow: Algorithm, 2005).

Orange Ukraine became the conductor of a distinctly Atlanticist, thalassocratic policy, directed against Russia, Eurasianism, tellurocracy, and integration, and durable ties were established between the two most active Atlanticists in the post-Soviet space, Saakashvili and Yushchenko. Geopolitical projects for the formation of a Baltic-Black Sea community arose, which, theoretically, comprised the countries of the Baltic, Ukraine, Moldova, Georgia, and the countries of Eastern Europe, Poland, and Hungary, who are, like the Baltic countries, members of NATO. This was a project for the establishment of a *cordon sanitaire* between Russia and Europe, built in accordance with the maps of the classical thalassocratic geopoliticians.

The positions of the other members of GUAM — Moldova and Azerbaijan — were not as radical and were largely dictated by local problems: Moscow's support for the mutinous Trans-Dniester Republic, which had announced its independence from Moldova in 1991, and the military collaboration between Russia and Armenia, that shared insoluble antagonisms with Azerbaijan over the occupation of Karabakh. The entire picture of the post-Soviet space in Putin's era was characterized by the transparent and distinct opposition of the civilization of Land (embodied in Russia and its allies) and the civilization of the Sea (embodied in the GUAM countries, led by Georgia and Ukraine). The Heartland strove to expand its sphere of influence in the CIS through processes of integration, while the USA strove through its satellites to limit the spread of Russian influence in this zone and to lock Russia within its own borders, and to gradually integrate the new countries surrounding it into NATO.

The battle between Eurasianism and Atlanticism within the post-Soviet space and the integrational processes of the CIS, on one hand, and the color revolutions on the other, was so evident that it is unlikely that any sober-minded Atlanticist could fail to understand what was put into action there. But the might of the Atlanticist networks of influence in Russia itself again made itself known: there was no broad social understanding of the processes taking place. Experts commented on particulars and details, losing sight of the most important aspects and consciously creating a distorted picture of events. Moreover, Putin's actions, aimed at deciding the problems of integration, were either suppressed or criticized, while candid Russophobia, which ruled in Georgia or Ukraine, was overlooked or reinterpreted neutrally.

The Russian media and the community of experts not only did not help Putin conduct his Eurasian campaign but, more often, prevented him from carrying it out. This was yet another paradox of Putin's period of rule.

The Munich Speech

Putin moved closer to the formulation of his geopolitical views in a consistent and non-contradictory way only toward the end of his second presidential term in 2007. His famous speech at the Munich Conference on Security Policy in 2007 became this formulation, although it was rather approximate and emotional. In this speech, Putin criticized the unipolar arrangement of the contemporary world system and described his vision of Russia's role in the contemporary world, considering present realities and threats. In contrast with the majority of his often evasive and internally inconsistent declarations, this speech, which has been called the "Munich speech," was distinguished by consistency and clarity. Putin seemed to break through the veil of the ambiguous and evasive postmodern demagoguery of the Atlanticist experts or of Surkov, which differentiated this speech from the majority of his previous programmatic statements. The main points of the Munich speech can be reduced to the following excerpts from it:

1. "For the contemporary world, the unipolar model is not only unacceptable, but altogether impossible."

2. "One state, the United States, has overstepped its national borders in every way. This is visible in the economic, political, cultural, and educational policies it imposes on other nations. "

3. "The sole mechanism for decision making about the use of military force as a last resort can only be the UN Charter."

4. "NATO advances its frontline forces to our state borders, but we, strictly fulfilling our agreement, do not react to these actions at all."

5. "What happened to those assurances given by our Western partners after the dissolution of the Warsaw Pact?"

6. "With one hand 'charitable aid' is given, but with the other, not only is economic backwardness preserved, but a profit is also collected."

7. "An attempt is being made to transform the Organization for Security and Cooperation in Europe (OSCE) into a vulgar instrument for guaranteeing the foreign policy interests of one or a group of countries against those of other countries."

8. "Russia is a country with a history of more than a thousand years, and it has practically always enjoyed the privilege of conducting an independent foreign policy. We are not about to change this tradition today."[162]

The Munich speech could well be taken as a fully-fledged strategic directive. The first point openly rejects the unipolar world order; it challenges the existing state of affairs and contests the world system that took shape after the fall of the USSR. This is quite a revolutionary statement, which can be regarded as the loud voice of the Heartland. In the second point, we are talking about a direct critique of the USA's policy as the hegemon of the thalassocratic strategy on a world scale and the censure of their supranational, aggressive activities. Both points, the first and the second, comprise a platform for a consistent and well-founded anti-Americanism.

---

162 Vladimir Putin, "Statement and Discussion at the Munich Conference on Security Policy," at archive.kremlin.ru/appears/2007/02/10/1737_type63374type63376type63377type63381type82634_118097.shtml

The third point is a proposal for a return to the Yalta model, expressed in the era of bipolarity by the UN. This was a "protective" response to the numerous appeals by the Americans to reform the UN or to repudiate its structure altogether as failing to correspond to the new balance of power, calling for its replacement by a new organization led by the USA and its vassals (similar to Mackinder's project of a "league of democracies").[163]

In the fourth point, Putin unambiguously criticizes the spread of NATO to the East, interpreting this process in the only possible way (from the point of view of Russia's national interests and responsible geopolitical analysis). Putin makes it clear that he is not a victim of the "liberal-democratic" demagoguery that tries to cover up the expansion of the West, and that he looks at things soberly.

The fifth point accuses the West of not fulfilling the promises it made to Gorbachev when he unilaterally cut short the Soviet military presence in Europe. That is, he faults thalassocracy for playing by the logic of double standards during the 1980s.

The sixth point condemns the economic strategy of the Western countries in the Third World, which, with the help of the World Bank and the International Monetary Fund, ruins developing countries under the guise of economic aid and subordinates them to their own political and economic domination.[164] Essentially, this is a call to the Third World to seek an alternative to existing liberal politics.

In the seventh point, Putin indicates that various European structures (in particular, the OSCE) do not serve European interests, but are instruments of the USA's aggressive policy and exert pressure on Russia in the political, energy, and economic spheres, contradicting the interests of the European countries themselves.

---

163 John McCain, "America Must Be a Good Role Model," in *Financial Times* (March 18, 2008).

164 John Perkins, *Confessions of an Economic Hit Man* (San Francisco: Berrett-Koehler Publishers, 2004).

Quintessential is the eighth point, which declares that Russia is a great world power that intends from now to conduct an *independent, self-reliant policy* and is ready to return to its traditional function as the core of the "civilization of Land" and a bastion of tellurocracy. Putin essentially announced that the idea that history has ended and that the Sea has at last conquered the Land is premature; the Land still exists, it is present, and it is ready to make itself loudly known.

The reaction to Putin's Munich speech in the West and the USA was extremely negative. The majority of Atlanticists and experts began to speak of a renewal of the "Cold War." Putin showed that he realizes that *the great war of continents has not ceased* and that today we are only in its next stage. After this, many Western strategists finally began to see Putin as the embodiment of a geopolitical adversary and the traditional image of the "Russian enemy," which had formed during the history of the geopolitical confrontation between Sea and Land.

After such a frank proclamation of his position on an international level, it was logical to suppose that Vladimir Putin, discarding his masks, would give a systematic character to these declarations, put them at the basis of his future strategy, ground a foreign policy doctrine on that foundation, and apply its main principles to the sphere of domestic policy. But nothing of the sort occurred. In Russia itself, people did not speak of the Munich speech for long. No significant discussions or debates were held. It did not affect the position of the Atlanticist networks at all, and it did not lead to any consistent national policy.

We can only guess why so striking a declaration was quickly stifled by technical, bureaucratic routine.

If we grant that Putin spoke sincerely and deliberately in his Munich speech, then, in contrast with how little resonance his words received in Russia itself and how little they affected domestic and foreign policy, we must think that he is a continentalist, a Eurasianist, and a supporter of strong governmental authority, but among a dense ring of Atlanticist,

American agents of influence, effectively sabotaging those of his serious initiatives which might harm their overseas masters.

Operation Medvedev

This ambiguity in Putin's geopolitical policy, continental and tellurocratic overall, but also containing contradictions in the form of influential units of the Atlanticist network at the highest levels of government, was shown in Putin's choice of his successor, Dmitry Medvedev, in March 2008. On one hand, Medvedev was a constant colleague of Putin in the various stages of his political career, and this alone should have ensured the similarity of their political and geopolitical attitudes. On the other hand, Medvedev's political image was openly liberal and pro-Western. This combination created an internal contradiction between tellurocracy and thalassocracy that was much more acute and salient than in the political line of Putin himself. In advancing Medvedev as his successor, Putin further accented the inconsistency of Russia's position in the world. Medvedev's Westernism and liberalism were not only obvious, but were also emphasized in every way possible from the moment that he was finally named as the presidential candidate from "Putin's party."

Already on the eve of his selection, Medvedev entrusted the elaboration of the main strategy of his foreign and domestic policy to the Institute of Russia's Contemporary Development (INSOR). This Institute had been established by the Russian Union of Industrialists and Entrepreneurs and was an organization uniting Russia's most influential and richest oligarchs under the leadership of the ultraliberal and unambiguously pro-American public figures I. Yurgens[165] and E. Gontmakher,[166] famous for their criticisms of Putin from an Atlanticist position; Medvedev himself became the head of the Board of Trustees of INSOR.

If we compare Putin's main strategy with the projects of INSOR, then we receive a complete and radical contradiction, aggravated by the INSOR ideologues' open criticisms of Putin and his policies. After Medvedev took office on November 15, 2008, he visited the headquarters of the CFR in New York,[167] an unprecedented event for a leader of Russia, providing evidence of the active Atlanticist, globalist, and hegemonic position of this influential organization.

It is significant that, through the authorized representative of the CFR, the oligarch Mikhail Fridman[168] (one of the members of the "Seven Bankers" of 1996), the Vice Premier of the Russian Federation, Sergei Ivanov, also established close ties with the CFR, speaking twice at it, on January 13, 2005[169] and again on April 4, 2011;[170] Ivanov was earlier regarded as a possible successor to Putin, as was Medvedev.

It is obvious that Putin consciously sanctioned this relation with the headquarters of Atlanticism and its most avant-garde, advanced structures and clearly understood the significance of the liberalism and Westernism of his successor. Putin, who consistently carried out a policy of strengthening Russian sovereignty and outlined his foreign policy in his Munich speech,

---

165 Igor Yurgens (b. 1952) is Vice President of the Russian Union of Industrialists and Entrepreneurs (RUIE) and is Chairman of the Institute of Contemporary Development, and has been called the 'voice of the oligarchs'.—Ed.

166 Yevgeny Gontmakher (b. 1953) was the Vice President of the RUIE and is currently the Deputy Director of the Institute of World Economics and International Relations at the Russian Academy of Sciences.—Ed.

167 www.cfr.org/us-strategy-and-politics/conversation-dmitry-medvedev-video/p17779

168 Mikhail Fridman (b. 1964) was one of the founders of the Alfa Group, one of the largest consortiums in post-Soviet Russia. In 2014 Forbes estimated him to be the second wealthiest person in Russia.—Ed.

169 www.cfr.org/global-governance/world-21st-century-addressing-new-threats-challenges-video/p8742, www.cfr.org/russian-fed/world-21st-century-addressing-new-threats-challenges/p7611

170 www.cfr.org/russian-fed/conversation-sergey-b-ivanov-video/p24578

also deliberately demonstrated a certain loyalty to Atlanticist projects. He not only kept the vast network of thalassocracy's agents of influence in place, but also made it clear through his choice of successor (including also S. B. Ivanov) that he was ready to implement a political line utterly different from the one that he has declared.

And again, it is not difficult to guess the reasons behind such a double game and its actual geopolitical purpose. However, when a man with nominally Atlanticist, globalist, and liberal attitudes and views becomes the leader of a country, and this happens solely thanks to Putin and his will, this transcends the possibility of Western influence and becomes something simply inexplicable for a figure such as Putin.

The solution to such a tactical approach was given at the United Russia party conference on September 24, 2011, when Medvedev announced that he was not running for a second term and proposed that Putin run again for President. Geopolitically, the picture was cleared up, and "Operation Medvedev" proved nothing other than an attempt to distract the West and win time for Putin's legal return to the presidential seat. And during Medvedev's rule, no critical concessions were made to Atlanticism, despite many declarations and a series of purely symbolic steps.

Saakashvili's Assault on Tskhinvali and the Russia-Georgian War of 2008

The Russia-Georgian War in August 2008 was an extremely important geopolitical event. Two of Georgia's administrative zones with a mixed population, where Ossetians predominated in South Ossetia and Abkhazians in Abkhazia, declared themselves to be politically autonomous regions. After the announcement that Georgia was giving up its membership in the USSR on April 9, 1991, they disagreed with this decision and, in turn, decided to forgo their membership in Georgia. Georgia did not agree with this and began military operations to keep Abkhazia and South Ossetia within its borders.

Georgian troops invaded Abkhazia in 1992 after Shevardnadze came to power and the previous President, Zviad Gamsakhurdia, was overthrown. In the first stage, they were successful in seizing Sukhumi and advancing all the way to Gagra. But later, relying on volunteers from the Republic of the Northern Caucasus and military, economic and diplomatic aid from Russia, the Abkhazians managed to reestablish control over Sukhumi by the end of 1993 and to fight off the Georgians. Meanwhile, the Georgians retained control over the territories of the Kodori Valley, which the Abkhazians considered a part of Abkhazia. Overall, this situation was preserved unchanged until August 2008.

Throughout 1991, South Ossetia was an arena for military operations. On January 19, 1992, there was a referendum on the question of "government independence and/or unification with North Ossetia" in South Ossetia. A majority of the participants in the referendum supported this proposal. After a lull, military operations in South Ossetia resumed in the spring of 1992, brought about by a *coup d'etat* and a civil war in Georgia. Under pressure from Russia, Georgia began negotiations, which ended on June 24, 1992, with the signing of the Sochi Agreement on the Principles of the Settlement of the Conflict. On July 14, 1992, there was a cease-fire, and the Mixed Peacekeeping Forces (SSPM) were introduced into the conflict zone to separate the opposing sides. After 1992 and until 2008, South Ossetia was a *de facto* independent government and had its own constitution and government symbols. The Georgian authorities considered it, as before, to be administrative unit, the Tskhinvali region.

Geopolitically, Abkhazia and South Ossetia were pro-Russian and anti-Georgian, which, because of Georgia's Atlanticist orientation, implied their Eurasian, continental, land-based and *tellurocratic* policy. When Mikhail Saakashvili came to power in 2003 on a wave of nationalist sentiments, it intensified the antagonisms between Tbilisi, Abkhazia, and South Ossetia even more, as Saakashvili's radical Atlanticism was openly leading to an escalation with the pro-Russian orientation of Sukhumi and Tskhinvali.

Saakashvili's promise to his constituency was to reestablish the territorial integrity of Georgia and remove the pro-Russian enclaves on its territory. In this, Saakashvili relied on economic and military aid from the USA and NATO countries.

For five years, the Georgian side actively prepared for new military actions and began an operation to seize South Ossetia on August 7, 2008. On the night of August 8, rocket fire on Tskhinvali began from "Grad" launchers, and Georgian troops began their assault on the city using tanks. The same day, they seized the city and began to exterminate the population. Georgian troops also shelled a contingent of Russian peacekeepers, causing significant casualties. According to international precepts, this meant that Georgia had declared war on Russia through the conduct of military operations against the regular armed forces of a foreign state.

In response, Moscow led a military contingent into South Ossetia on September 8 through the Roki tunnel, and on September 9 Russian troops approached Tskhinvali, engaged the Georgian troops and began to liberate both the city and the entirety of South Ossetia from the Georgian occupation.

Simultaneously, Russian troops entered the territory of the Kodori Valley and destroyed the Georgians' military bases there.

Finding themselves at war with Georgia, Russian troops started to advance to Tbilisi, the capital of Georgia, but after marching deep into the territory of their enemy, they later retreated and returned to the borders of South Ossetia and Abkhazia. Afterwards, Dmitry Medvedev explained that the cessation of this incursion into Georgia, which had every chance of ending in Russia's victory, was his personal achievement.

On August 26, 2008, Russia recognized the independence of South Ossetia and Abkhazia in the borders then existing.

Thereby, in practice after Medvedev's coming to power, Russia continued to follow Putin's policy of strengthening Russia's sovereignty when it was seriously tested by an encounter with an attack by Atlanticist forces within tellurocratic Russia's zone of strategic influence. Russian forces even went beyond the borders of the Russian Federation proper for the first time since the fall of the USSR without fearing Western pressure or threats from the USA.

It is revealing that the entire Atlanticist network of agents in Russia during that period opposed this turn of events in unison, and insisted on Russia's non-interference in the Georgia-Ossetia conflict. They later took all possible actions to prevent Moscow's recognition of the independence of these countries.

The events of August 2008 were a tense moment in the great war of continents, when the forces of the civilization of the Sea (standing behind Saakashvili) and the civilization of Land (Russia and the Republics of South Ossetia and Abkhazia) collided in a tough confrontation; this time, the civilization of Land scored an unambiguous victory. This victory had a significant military dimension, since the Georgian troops were defeated despite being fitted with the latest NATO equipment and having American instructors. Besides that, this was a political and diplomatic victory: Russia was successful in avoiding confrontation with the West and in preventing the rise of a harsh anti-Russian coalition. Lastly, the victory was informational, as the Russian media (in radical contrast with the First Chechen War) synchronously transmitted a state-patriotic, pro-Ossetian position, shared by a majority of the population.

Thus, the recently selected President Dmitry Medvedev showed himself to be a politician in the face of a harsh challenge from the Atlanticist powers, putting into practice (and not by words) an unambiguously *tellurocratic decision* in a difficult situation, based solely on an adequate appraisal of Russian interests. This development seemed to illuminate Putin's true strategy: under the guise of a liberal and pro-Western course of Russian politics, Putin's strategy for strengthening Russia's sovereignty and asserting its geopolitical interests in the post-Soviet space was retained.

It is significant that the Atlanticist lobby, called into full combat readiness during this affair, failed to exert the slightest influence on the decisions of the President, the Premier, and the leaders of the armed forces (if we do not count Medvedev's refusal to seize Tbilisi, the expedience of which could be interpreted in different ways).

The Reset and the Return to Atlanticism

But after August 2008, the events of which should logically have led to a renewal of confrontation with the West, entirely different processes began in Russia's foreign policy. Medvedev announced a policy of closer relations with the West and especially with the USA, a policy of modernizing and Westernizing Russian society, and a policy of deepening liberal reforms. This policy was supported by President Barack Obama. Although it evoked indignation in the USA and in the West, the Russia-Georgia war did not become a serious argument in favor of beginning a new phase in the anti-Russian campaign. Everyone in the USA understood that Russia had won a tactical victory, but for whatever reasons they went on to soften the situation and did not sharply raise the temperature of the confrontation.

In this period the process began that received the name "reset" in the international press, signifying closer relations between Russia and the USA after a period of cooling connected with the Putin era. The "reset" proposed the harmonization of both countries' regional interests and the implementation of common operations when both had similar regional aims. In practice this was expressed in the following ways:

- Russia's support for US and NATO military operations in Afghanistan;
- the signing of the New Strategic Arms Reduction Treaty (START) for the reduction of strategic arms;
- Russia's cancellation of the delivery of certain kinds of armaments to Iran;

• Russia's support for US and NATO policies in the Arab world (in particular, the renunciation of its veto in the UN Security Council resolution on Libya, which led to US and NATO military intervention into
  the country and the overthrow of the Gaddafi regime).

Besides these steps, which overall gave some concrete advantages to the
USA and practically nothing to Russia, there were no serious movements
in Russian-American relations during Medvedev's presidency. The USA
continued to expand its anti-ballistic missile defense program in Europe,
despite Russia's protests, changing its plans only because of the results of
the negotiations with the directly affected countries in Eastern Europe.
Moreover, the USA put parts of its anti-ballistic missile defense systems in
Turkey, close to the Russian border.

    Meanwhile, in the opinion of Putin and Russia's military leadership,
the entire European anti-ballistic missile system theoretically had as its
goal only an anti-Russian strategic program for the restraint of Russia and
could, under certain circumstances, serve offensive purposes. Not only did
the "reset" not stop American initiatives of European anti-ballistic missile
defense; it did not even slow them.

    A geopolitical analysis of the "reset" can be reduced to the following:
without a common enemy (a third force) for the civilization of the Sea,
which pretends to be global, and since the civilization of Land finds itself
in a reduced and weakened condition, *there are not and cannot be any common, serious strategic aims.* Under these conditions, given the asymmetrical
nature of their power-related, economic, and military relations, a search
for the points of contact can lead objectively only to the further *one-sided
process of Russia's de-sovereignization*, as happened in the era of Gorbachev
and Yeltsin, and to the curtailment of that course that Putin emphasized
during his rule. Judging by certain declarations, the projects of Medvedev's
INSOR, and the information-management of the "reset" in the Russian

media, the entire content of this process could be understood in precisely this way. And perhaps Western strategists had this attitude toward it, while delays in fulfilling irreversible steps favoring the West were due to the fact that the new President had "not yet freed himself entirely from the influence of Putin, who brought him to power." It was true, as March 2012 approached, that more and more Atlanticist analysts began to express doubts about the seriousness of the intentions of Medvedev and his pro-American, ultraliberal circle, and about his independence. Voices were heard suggesting that Medvedev's presidency was nothing other than a means to gain time before the inevitable and straightforward confrontation, which would become inescapable if Putin were to return to power. But the hope that the Russian President-reformer might remain for a second term kept the West from exerting more serious pressure on Russia. According to some sources,[171] American Vice President Joe Biden, during his visit to Moscow in the spring of 2011, tried to interfere in Russia's domestic policies by openly calling on Putin not to run for another term, warning of a "color revolution" similar to those that had occurred in the Arab world in 2011.

If we turn our attention away from this formal perspective of American pressure on Russia and the apparent readiness of Russia under Medvedev to take irreversible actions in this direction, which would have sharply broken with Putin's course, were not undertaken. Overall, all the steps toward the USA and NATO that Medvedev made had a purely declarative character or affected only the secondary aspects of the complete strategy. Russia's losses during this period were insignificant and incomparable with those that the country incurred under Gorbachev and Yeltsin.

After Putin's decision to return to the Kremlin and Medvedev's own support for this decision, no doubts remained for anyone that this had been a tactical move.

---

171 "Biden tried to dissuade Putin from participating in the election," *Newsland*, Sofia Sardzevaldze, 3 Dec 2011, www.newsland.ru/news/detail/id/653351/

The Eurasian Union

Putin's programmatic text, "The Eurasian Union: A Path to Success and Prosperity," published in the newspaper *Izvestia* on October 3, 2011, was extremely significant. In this text, Putin declared a landmark in the integration of the post-Soviet space, first on an economic level, and then on a political one (about which, it is true, he only hints).

Beyond economic integration, Putin described a higher — geopolitical and political — aim: the future creation on the space of Northern Eurasia of a new, supranational organization, built on civilizational commonality. As the European Union, uniting countries and societies related to European civilization, began with the "European Coal and Steel Community" to gradually develop into a new supra-governmental organization, so too would the Eurasian Union take on a supranational character, declared by Putin to be a long-term, historic goal.

The idea of a Eurasian Union was worked out in two countries simultaneously in the early 1990s: in Kazakhstan by President N. A. Nazarbayev[172] and in Russia by the Eurasian Movement.[173] In Moscow in 1994, Nazarbayev voiced the idea of this project of the political integration of the post-Soviet space, and even proposed the development of a constitution for a Eurasian Union similar to that of the European Union. And, for its part, the idea of a Eurasian Union was actively elaborated by the Eurasian Movement in Russia, continuing in the line of the first Russian Eurasianists, who had laid the foundations for this political philosophy. The creation of a Eurasian Union became the principal historic, political, and ideological aim of the Russian Eurasianists, as this project embodied all the primary values, ideals, and horizons of Eurasianism as a complete political philosophy.

---

172 Alexander Dugin, *Nursultan Nazarbayev's Eurasian Mission* (Moscow: Eurasia Publishing, 2004).

173 *The Eurasian Mission: Policy Papers of the International Eurasian Movement* (Moscow, 2005). [English edition: *Eurasian Mission: An Introduction to Neo-Eurasianism* (London: Arktos, 2014). The Eurasian Movement is Alexander Dugin's own organization.—Ed.].

Thus Putin, turning his attention to the Eurasian Union, emphasized a political idea imbued with deep political and geopolitical significance. The Eurasian Union, as the concrete embodiment of the Eurasian project, contains three levels at once: the planetary, the regional, and the domestic.

1. On a planetary scale, we are talking about the establishment, in the place of a unipolar or "nonpolar" (global) world, of a multipolar model, where only a powerful, integrated regional organization can be a whole (exceeding even the largest states by its scale and economic, military-strategic, and energy potential).

2. On a regional scale, we are talking about the creation of an integrated organization capable of being a pole of a multipolar world. In the West, the European Union can act as such a project of integration. For Russia, this means the integration of the post-Soviet space into a single strategic bloc.

3. Domestically, Eurasianism means the assertion of strategic centralism, rejecting even the suggestion of the presence of prototypes of national statehood in the subjects of the Federation. It also implies a broad program for strengthening the cultural, linguistic, and social identities of those ethnoses that comprise Russia's traditional composition.

Putin repeatedly spoke of multipolarity in his assessments of the international situation. Putin started to speak about the necessity of distinguishing the "nation" (a political formation) from the "ethnos" in domestic policy in the spring of 2011, which means that the Eurasian model was adopted at this time.[174]

Thus, Eurasianism can be taken as Putin's general strategy for the future, and the unambiguous conclusion follows from this that the strategy of Russia's return to its geopolitical, continental function as the Heartland will be clarified, consolidated, and carried out.

---

174 Alexander Dugin, *Ethnosociology* (Moscow: Academic Project, 2011).

The Outcomes of the Geopolitics of the 2000s

Today it is difficult to predict precisely how the geopolitical situation will unfold over the next few years, while the general assessment of Putin's geopolitical line will depend on this in many ways. If Putin is successful in securing the position of Russia's sovereignty and begins an effective policy of creating a multipolar world in all its concurrent directions and, even more importantly, irreversibly re-establishing Russia's strategic role in the global context, his success will affect not only the future, but also our assessment of the true significance of the recent past from the year 2000 until today.

For now, we can state that *Russia has not yet passed the point of no return,* and through some circumstance or another, Putin's course can prove to be both what it looks like today and what Putin himself gave utterance to in his Munich speech. Or it can prove to be something entirely different, a wavering or temporary deceleration along the path of strengthening American hegemony and a unipolar world at the cost of the civilization of Land and the ultimate weakening and destruction of Russia itself.

For now, the question remains: how are we to understand all of Putin's geopolitically ambiguous and inconsistent actions? This includes both the strengthening of sovereignty and the preservation of Atlanticism's network of influential agents; the confrontation with the USA and the call to reject unipolarity, while supporting American projects in Afghanistan (and Russia's elimination from the Arab world and the processes occurring there); closer relations with countries oriented toward multipolarity (China, Brazil, Iran), and the "reset." Which of these will prove dominant? Which is merely a tactical maneuver and disinformation? Under the current circumstances, this question cannot receive an unambiguous answer, and geopolitical analysis in this case cannot be entirely reliable, since the most important processes are unfolding around us now, and no one today can speak with certainty about their true significance and substance.

The geopolitical cycle that Putin began in the autumn of 1999 immediately after he came to power is as yet unfinished. In its main characteristics, it is a movement in an entirely different direction from the vector of Russian geopolitics during the second half of the 1980s until the end of the 1990s (the Gorbachev-Yeltsin era). Putin decelerated the movement, which was by inertia leading inevitably to Russia's complete weakening and its ultimate geopolitical destruction. He also began the complicated maneuvers necessary to reverse this trend. But this maneuver has not been brought to its logical end. The historical fate of the government and the civilization of Land as the whole — the Heartland, Russia-Eurasia — remains open.

CHAPTER V

The Point of Bifurcation in the Geopolitical History of Russia

To complete our summary of Russia's geopolitical history, we can present its general results.

First, the spatial logic of the history of Russian statehood is unambiguously revealed. This logic can be summarized as *expansion to the natural borders of northeast Eurasia, Turan, with the prospect of extending its zone of influence beyond its boundaries, perhaps on a planetary scale.* This is the main conclusion that we can draw from a consideration of all periods of Russian political history, from the emergence of Kievan Rus up to today's Russian Federation and the post-Soviet space.

Initially, Rus was formed in western Turan, where the imperial forms of other Eurasian peoples had existed, including Scythians, Sarmatians, Huns, Turks, and Goths. From the Kievan center, an integration of concentric circles on all sides occured, leading to the *first embodiment* of the Russian state, whose outer limits circumscribed the resplendent campaigns of Svyatoslav.[175] Later, this geopolitical form was strengthened and slightly altered, losing control over some territories and gaining it over others.

---

175 Svyatoslav I was the Grand Prince of Kiev from 945 until 972, who conquered wide swaths of land and defeated several rival kingdoms in the Slavic territories.—Ed.

Then, this exemplary form was crushed in the Appanage principality (*udel'nie kniazhestva*), and a wearisome fight for the throne of the Grand Duchy of Moscow[176] began, in the course of which there gradually took shape *two poles of attraction: the Eastern* (the Rostov-Suzdal, later the Vladimir-Suzdal, principality) and the *Western* (Galicia and Volhynia).

After the Mongolian conquests, Rus lost its independence and represented mostly the *eastern part*, where the Grand Duchy throne was fixed. On the other hand, integration with the "Golden Horde" put Rus in the gigantic and genuinely continental Turanic empire, the civilization of Land in all its geopolitical and sociological dimensions. If Turanic influence was previously spread through the Eastern-Slavic tribes, now the experience of Turanic statehood was grafted onto the political organism that had formed and was capable of learning the lesson of the Eurasian empire and becoming a new imperial center.

Western Rus was drawn into the orbit of the Grand Duchy of Lithuania, and this predetermined its fate, especially after the Krevsk Union of 1385.[177]

In the fifteenth century, after the collapse of the Horde, Muscovite Rus began the slow path not only to reestablish the Kievan state, but also to integrate all Turan, which had been embodied in a new and this time Russian version of integrated Eurasia, around her core, the continental Heartland. From now on, Russian geopolitical history finally sets upon the path of a Eurasian vector and a completed tellurocracy, and proceeds toward the establishment of a world-scale civilization of Land.

In all the following stages, from the fifteenth century to the end of the twentieth century, Rus continued its spiral expansion across the continent's natural borders. Sometimes the territory of Rus contracted for a short period, but only to expand again in the next stage. Thus beat the geopolitical heart of the Heartland, pushing its power, its population, its troops,

---

176 The Grand Duchy of Moscow was established in 1283 and lasted until 1587, being the predecessor of the Czardom of Russia.—Ed.

177 The Krevsk Union brought about the unification of the Grand Duchy of Lithuania with the Kingdom of Poland.—Ed.

and other forms of influence to the outer edges of Eurasia, all the way to the coastal zone (Rimland). The living, beating, and growing heart of the world's land-based empire predetermines Rus-Russia's path toward the establishment of a world power and one of the two global poles of the world.

Under various ideologies and political systems, Russia moved toward world dominance, having firmly embarked on the path of establishing control over Eurasia from within and from the position of the center of the inner continent. From the end of the eighteenth century, it collided in its expansion with the British Empire, the embodiment of the global civilization of the Sea. In the twentieth century, this confrontation led smoothly, on an entirely new ideological level, into the twentieth century to a confrontation with the next global maritime pole, the USA. In the Soviet period, *the great war of continents* reached its apogee: the influence of the civilization of Land as the USSR extended far beyond the borders of the Russian Empire and beyond the borders of the Eurasian continent into Africa, Latin America, and Asia. *Precisely this vector of continental, and later global, expansion, carried out in the name of the Heartland, tellurocracy, and the civilization of Land, is the "spatial meaning" (Raumsinn) of Russian history.* All intermediate stages and all historical fluctuations and oscillations along this path were nothing other than the rotation of real historical events around a central geopolitical channel: retreats, roundabout maneuvers, and delays do not change the principal vector of Russian history.

Through this analysis of Russia's geopolitics, we can geopolitically assess today's state of affairs and mark out the vector of its geopolitical future.

It is clear that Russia's geopolitical position after Gorbachev's reforms, the collapse of the USSR, and the period of Yeltsin's rule is an almost catastrophic *step backwards* and a failure of the geopolitical matrix which was moving throughout the previous stages, without exception, toward spatial expansion. From the end of the 1980s, Russia started to swiftly lose its positions in the global space of the world, positions it had conquered with such difficulty and through so many deaths across many generations of the

Russian people. The losses we suffered at this time are not comparable with the Time of Troubles or with the results of the Brest-Litovsk treaty. Even the campaigns of Napoleon and Hitler, which brought countless deaths, were short, and territorial losses were swiftly restored and recovered, and sometimes even resulted in territorial gains. The uniqueness of today's geopolitical cycle lies precisely in this: it has lasted unusually long (for Russian history), its losses have not been compensated for by any acquisitions, and the catastrophic paralysis of the state's self-consciousness is not counterbalanced by any striking personalities, adequate leaders, or successful operations. This engenders a well-founded anxiety about the condition in which Russia finds itself today and apprehension over its future. The most dispassionate and impartial analysis of Russia's geopolitics shows that *today's position is a pathology*, a deviation from its natural, undeniable historical trajectory. We can consider the Mongolian invasions the sole analogy, resulting in its loss of independence for two centuries, but even that was compensated for by the fact that during this period Russia imbued the experience of Eurasian continental tellurocracy, a lesson it learned well and later used to establish global power. It is amazing how Gorbachev and his circle incompetently lost the "Cold War," not to mention how the naïve (not to say half-witted) reformers of the Yeltsin period were gladdened by the collapse of the USSR and the de-sovereignization of Russia, even allowing the establishment of foreign, Atlanticist control over the country, particularly if we compare this to the steady growth of territorial increases that occurred in the times of practically all the Czars without exception, and in all the cycles of the Soviet era. In the general ranks of Russian potentates, the names of Gorbachev and Yeltsin can only stand alongside the names of Yaropolk,[178] False Dmitry,[179] Shuysky,[180] or Kerensky. Their personalities and their politics were a complete and unmitigated *failure*.

The normalization of Russia's natural historical vector only occurred with Putin's coming to power, when the process of collapse, and thereby Russia's ultimate death, was stopped or at least postponed. But the contradictions of the Putin era and especially the period of Medvedev's rule, sometimes reminiscent in certain ways of the era of Gorbachev and Yeltsin, does not allow us to be sure that the recurrent trouble is behind and that Russia has entered its natural, continental Eurasian orbit again. We want to believe in this, but, alas, there are not yet enough grounds for such belief: all Putin's geopolitical reforms, positive in the highest degree, have one exceedingly important shortcoming: *they are not irreversible*. They have not passed the point of no return. They can anytime undergo the destructive processes that prevailed at the end of the Soviet era and in the democratic 1990s.

Russia's geopolitical future is questionable today, because its geopolitical present is debatable. In Russia itself, a hidden confrontation occurs among the political elite between the new Westernism (Atlanticism) and gravitation toward the constants of Russian history (which necessarily gives us Eurasianism). We can draw a few conclusions from this about coming geopolitical processes.

The duration of this deep geopolitical crisis, drawn out longer than all previous ones, and its insurmountability up to today, indicates that the geopolitical construct of the Heartland finds itself in a confused state, reflected not only in strategy and foreign policy, but also in the quality of the elite and in the overall condition of society.

---

178 Yaropolk Izyaslavich was the King of Rus from 1076 and 1078. He was accused of negligence and the people of Kiev revolted against him when he was a prince.—Ed.

179 'False Dmitry' is the name applied to a number of pretenders to the throne of Russia during the Time of Troubles, who claimed to be descendants of Ivan the Terrible.—Ed.

180 Princes Ivan and Andrey Shuysky ruled Rus during Ivan the Terrible's youth. They were regarded as arrogant and incompetent rulers. Andrey was eventually thrown into a cell with hungry dogs, which devoured him.—Ed.

Consequently, serious and perhaps extraordinary efforts across many spheres are needed to get out of this situation, including social and ideological *mobilization*. But this, in its turn, demands a strong-willed and energetic personality at the head of government, a new type of ruling elite and a new form of ideology. Only in this case will the main geopolitical vector of Russian history be extended into the future.

If we grant that this will happen presently, we can guess that Russia will take the lead in building a multipolar world and will embark on the creation of a versatile system of global alliances. These will be aimed at undermining American hegemony, and Russia will emerge anew as a planetary power in the organization of a concrete multipolar model on principally new foundations, proposing a broad pluralism of civilizations, values, economic structures, and so forth. In this case, Russia's influence will grow rapidly, and the basic vector of its development toward being a world power will be renewed. Precisely such a scenario can be placed at the basis of a non-contradictory geopolitical doctrine for Russia, which can be called on to provide it with a plan to remain faithful to its historical and civilizational ambitions in the future and its "spatial meaning."

But we cannot rule out that events will unfold according to a different script and that the protracted crisis will continue. In this case, Russia's sovereignty will again weaken, its territorial integrity will be questioned, and the processes of the degeneration of the ruling elite and the depressed condition of the broad masses will corrode society from within. In tandem with effective policies carried out by the civilization of the Sea and its networks of influence in Russia, this could lead to the most destructive consequences. In this case, it will be pointless to speak of Russian geopolitics.

In our society, some support the view that this time, Russia need not have global or imperial ambitions, thinking that the country is in no condition to allow this; but they also agree that it must not fall apart and degrade, as in the previous stage. Supporters of this point of view, however, do not take into account that in contemporary circumstances, to try to preserve our sovereignty at today's level while not making any attempt to expand and strengthen it cannot succeed for long, since the USA and the civilization of the Sea have already overtaken Russia for the most part. When the separation between the two becomes critical, the forces of Atlanticism will not hesitate to strike a decisive blow against their primary adversary in the great war of continents. All discussions that claim that the West no longer views Russia as a rival and is only concerned with the "Islamic threat" or with the growth of China's potential are nothing but a diversionary tactic, and weapons in an information war. Every American strategist who received a good education cannot fail to understand the laws of geopolitics; cannot fail to know Mahan, Mackinder, Spykman, and Bowman, and cannot ignore Brzezinski or Kissinger. *The American elite are perfectly aware of their Atlanticist nature* and remember the important formula of the geopoliticians about how to achieve global dominance: "Who rules Eurasia rules the whole world." Therefore, geopolitically, it is unfounded and empty to hope that Russia will be able to preserve itself in the reduced and regional form in which it now exists, after repudiating mobilization, a new round of expansion, and any participation in world-historical processes on behalf of the civilization of Land (expressed today in the principle of multipolarity). In this is the meaning of the entirely fitting formula, "Russia will either be great or will not be at all."[181] Russia will not be able to become a "normal" country by inertia and without effort. *If it will not begin a new cycle of ascension, it will be helped in entering a new round of decline.* And if this happens, then it will be impossible to say on what stage the recurrent cycle of fall, crisis, and catastrophe will end. We cannot rule out the disappearance of our country from the map; after all, the great war of continents is the genuine form of war, in which the price of defeat is disappearance. We should not concentrate too much on this gloomy prospect, since the future is open and largely depends on efforts undertaken today. As the Italian writer and

---

181 Alexander Dugin, *Russian Thing* (Moscow: Arctogaia, 2001). (Putin also reportedly said this at a conference on Ukrainian integration into the CIS in 2003.—Ed.)

political thinker Curzio Malaparte said, "Nothing is lost until everything is lost."[182] Therefore, we should look toward the future with reasonable optimism and create this great-continental Eurasian future for Russia with our own hands.

---

182 This is a paraphrase of a statement that occurs in Malaparte's book, *Coup d'Etat: The Technique of Revolution* (New York: E. P. Dutton, 1932).—Ed.

INDEX

OTHER BOOKS PUBLISHED BY ARKTOS

OTHER BOOKS PUBLISHED BY ARKTOS

OTHER BOOKS PUBLISHED BY ARKTOS

Roderick Kaine	*Smart and SeXy*
Peter King	*Here and Now*
	Keeping Things Close
	On Modern Manners
James Kirkpatrick	*Conservatism Inc.*
Ludwig Klages	*The Biocentric Worldview*
	Cosmogonic Reflections
	The Science of Character
Andrew Korybko	*Hybrid Wars*
Pierre Krebs	*Guillaume Faye: Truths & Tributes*
	Fighting for the Essence
Julien Langella	*Catholic and Identitarian*
John Bruce Leonard	*The New Prometheans*
Stephen Pax Leonard	*The Ideology of Failure*
	Travels in Cultural Nihilism
William S. Lind	*Reforging Excalibur*
	Retroculture
Pentti Linkola	*Can Life Prevail?*
H. P. Lovecraft	*The Conservative*
Norman Lowell	*Imperium Europa*
Richard Lynn	*Sex Differences in Intelligence*
John MacLugash	*The Return of the Solar King*
Charles Maurras	*The Future of the Intelligentsia &*
	For a French Awakening
John Harmon McElroy	*Agitprop in America*
Michael O'Meara	*Guillaume Faye and the Battle of Europe*
	New Culture, New Right
Michael Millerman	*Beginning with Heidegger*
Maurice Muret	*The Greatness of Elites*
Brian Anse Patrick	*The NRA and the Media*
	Rise of the Anti-Media
	The Ten Commandments of Propaganda
	Zombology
Tito Perdue	*The Bent Pyramid*
	Journey to a Location
	Lee
	Morning Crafts
	Philip
	The Sweet-Scented Manuscript
	William's House (vol. 1–4)
John K. Press	*The True West vs the Zombie Apocalypse*
Raido	*A Handbook of Traditional Living* (vol. 1–2)
Claire Rae Randall	*The War on Gender*
P R Reddall	*Towards Awakening*

OTHER BOOKS PUBLISHED BY ARKTOS

STEVEN J. ROSEN	*The Agni and the Ecstasy*
	The Jedi in the Lotus
NICHOLAS ROONEY	*Talking to the Wolf*
RICHARD RUDGLEY	*Barbarians*
	Essential Substances
	Wildest Dreams
ERNST VON SALOMON	*It Cannot Be Stormed*
	The Outlaws
WERNER SOMBART	*Traders and Heroes*
PIERO SAN GIORGIO	*CBRN*
	Giuseppe
	Survive the Economic Collapse
SRI SRI RAVI SHANKAR	*Celebrating Silence*
	Know Your Child
	Management Mantras
	Patanjali Yoga Sutras
	Secrets of Relationships
GEORGE T. SHAW (ED.)	*A Fair Hearing*
FENEK SOLÈRE	*Kraal*
	Reconquista
OSWALD SPENGLER	*The Decline of the West*
	Man and Technics
RICHARD STOREY	*The Uniqueness of Western Law*
TOMISLAV SUNIC	*Against Democracy and Equality*
	Homo Americanus
	Postmortem Report
	Titans are in Town
ASKR SVARTE	*Gods in the Abyss*
HANS-JÜRGEN SYBERBERG	*On the Fortunes and Misfortunes*
	of Art in Post-War Germany
ABIR TAHA	*Defining Terrorism*
	The Epic of Arya (2nd ed.)
	Nietzsche's Coming God, or the
	Redemption of the Divine
	Verses of Light
JEAN THIRIART	*Europe: An Empire of 400 Million*
BAL GANGADHAR TILAK	*The Arctic Home in the Vedas*
DOMINIQUE VENNER	*For a Positive Critique*
	The Shock of History
HANS VOGEL	*How Europe Became American*
MARKUS WILLINGER	*A Europe of Nations*
	Generation Identity
ALEXANDER WOLFHEZE	*Alba Rosa*
	Rupes Nigra